"Monarchs need our help now more than ever. All of us can do our part by planting milkweed and nectar plants. This book can show you how to help and protect the monarch butterfly population."

~ **Holli Hearn,** monarch enthusiast and founder of "The Beautiful Monarch" Facebook group

"Kylee Baumle's passion for the monarch butterfly has inspired me to pay closer attention to making my own garden – and those of my clients – a haven for this gorgeous creature. Her valuable information, stunning photographs and stirring prose will inspire you to do the same."

~ **Jenny Peterson,** landscape designer and author of *The Cancer Survivor's Garden Companion,* co-author *of Indoor Plant Decor*

"Kylee Baumle is blessed with the magnificent obsession to be absolutely correct about everything she writes. Readers can rest assured that every fact within the pages of *The Monarch* has been subjected to the most rigorous research and analysis since Noah assigned seating on the ark."

~ **Steve Bender,** *Southern Living* magazine's "The Grumpy Gardener"

"Kylee not only shares her knowledge and passion about monarchs, but inspires us to join forces to preserve this important pollinator. She offers practical advice on how each person can make a difference to save this and other pollinators critical to our food supply and natural beauty."

~ **Melinda Myers,** horticulturist, author of numerous garden books, radio & tv host of Melinda's Garden Moments

*the*

# MONARCH

*the*

# MONARCH

*Saving Our
Most-Loved Butterfly*

**Kylee Baumle**

St. Lynn's press
Pittsburgh

## THE MONARCH
### Saving Our Most-Loved Butterfly

ISBN-13: 978-1-943366-17-0

Library of Congress Control Number: 2016958268
CIP information available upon request

First Edition, 2017

St. Lynn's Press . POB 18680 . Pittsburgh, PA 15236
412.466.0790 . www.stlynnspress.com

Book design – Holly Rosborough
Editor – Catherine Dees

Photo credits: All photos © Kylee Baumle, with the exception of the following:
page 28 – KC Angel; page 32 – Bob Peterson (Creative Commons – https://creativecommons.org/licenses/by/2.0);
page 33 – aecole2010 (Viceroy, Creative Commons by 2.0); page 34 – Renee/Monkeystyle3000 (Queen, Creative Commons by 2.0); page 39 – Canadian Geographic (Migration Map); page 41 – Luna sin estrellas (Creative Commons by 2.0); page 42 – Heather Spaulding (Creative Commons by 2.0); page 44 – Eneas De Troya (Creative Commons by 2.0); page 46 graph – Monarch Watch; page 54 left – Official White House Photo by Amanda Lucidon; page 54 (poster) – Monarch Watch; page 56 top – Forests for Monarchs; page 61 – U.S. Fish & Wildlife Service (Creative Commons by 2.0); pages 62-63 – Carol Pasternak; page 70 – Will Pollard (Poke Milkweed) (Creative Commons – https://creativecommons.org/licenses/by-sa/2.0); page 71 – Fritz Flohr Reynolds (Purple Milkweed – https://creativecommons.org/licenses/by-sa/2.0); page 71 – Larry McAfee, National Park Service (Showy Milkweed); pages 72 and 73 – Swallowtail Garden Seeds (White Milkweed, Green Milkweed); page 73 – Mikeumo (Antelope Horn Milkweed – Creative Commons by 2.0); page 76 top right – University of New Hampshire Library; page 76 bottom right – Westby Times; page 79 right – Holli Hearn; page 85 – S. Rae (Tachinid Fly – Creative Commons by 2.0; page 87 – Holli Hearn (Trichogramma Wasp); page 88 – Judy Gallagher (Chalcid Wasp – Creative Commons  by 2.0); page 91 – Edith Smith; page 103 – NASA;  page 124 – Jenna DeCraene; page 126 – Ellen Zachos; page 130 – Marcy Cunkelman; page 150 – David Moskowitz

Every effort has been made to obtain photo permissions.
Any omissions were purely unintentional and will be corrected in subsequent printings.

Printed in Canada
On certified FSC recycled paper using soy-based inks

This title and all of St. Lynn's Press books may be purchased for educational,
business or sales promotional use. For information please write:
Special Markets Department . St. Lynn's Press . POB 18680 . Pittsburgh, PA 15236

10 9 8 7 6 5 4 3 2 1

FOR

**HANNAH, ANTHONY AND MAVERICK –**

WITH WHOM I GET TO DISCOVER

THE WONDER OF LIFE ALL OVER AGAIN.

# Table of Contents

# Introduction

❀

## Where have all the butterflies gone?

It's a question I hear being asked quite a bit these days. And while it does seem like there are fewer butterflies than there used to be, none is more conspicuously absent than the monarch, the most recognizable butterfly in North America – and indisputably the most beloved. Not long ago, monarchs numbered in the billions, but in the last 20 years their population has dropped by 90%.

We know some of the reasons for this dramatic decline. The good news is we can do something about a number of them, and the even better news is, it isn't too late. In the pages that follow, we will take an intimate look at this iconic insect and learn that there are all kinds of things to love about it beyond its pretty face. The monarch is truly a wonder of nature.

I've been asked if it really matters if the monarch disappears, and whether or not we should care. The truth is that it *does* matter. There are reasons that we should care about this butterfly and they extend beyond the monarch itself. Perhaps the universe is using this beautiful creature to get our attention and draw us to more important matters. Maybe the monarch is merely the messenger in a world that is changing, and those changes aren't always beneficial to the earth and those of us who inhabit it.

I remember as a child, seeing monarchs flying around my mother's garden and my grandmother's too – sometimes chasing them, though never catching them. To me they looked like animated jewelry among the static beauty of the colorful blooms. They seemed to be the perfect accessory to a well-dressed garden.

Little did I know then that they had a greater purpose, as pollinators. And I was naively unaware of their astounding story of birth, growth, and metamorphosis inside an emerald green chrysalis, hidden away among the plants.

It wasn't until many years later – decades, actually – when I became what I call "a true gardener," that I learned of the even more amazing story behind the monarch. Its autumn journey south to Mexico, to a location that was known only to locals until 1975, earns it the distinction of having one of the longest insect migrations in the world.

There is much to learn about the monarch, and as a backyard gardener, like many of us, I'm learning more all the time. But even the most basic facts and knowledge about the monarch and its life cycle can be enough to draw you into its world and capture your heart. You'll soon find yourself caring more than you ever thought possible about this summer resident of the U.S. and Canada that spends its winters in Mexico.

This book has been written out of my own passion for the monarch butterfly and aims to share not only the fascinating story and astounding facts about it, but also how you can bring the monarch into your world in ways that are fun and beneficial for both you and this amazing butterfly. Yes, the North American population of monarchs is in peril, but I have great hope that that will change.

Margaret Mead once said, *"Never doubt that a small group of thoughtful, committed citizens can change the world. Indeed, it is the only thing that ever has."*

Imagine what we can do together. As the number of us who care about pollinators in general and monarchs in particular grows, and more of us are moved to do what we can to help, so will there be an increase in monarchs. I want my grandchildren and their grandchildren to be able to experience firsthand this wondrous creature – I'll bet you do, too.

Let's work together and do this!

*Kylee*

# ONE

# A STORY

❧

**Serendipity**: accidentally finding something wonderful while not looking for it.
~ **Adriana Law**

On a sunny day in **September 2006** – the 17th, to be exact – my mother and I were traveling down U.S. Route 30 on our way home to Ohio from a trip to Delaware. We were in western Pennsylvania when we noticed a small sign by the side of the road indicating that the United Flight 93 Memorial was just two miles to the south.

It had been five years since that tragedy, and being that it was September, it had been on our minds. We decided to turn off and pay our respects to those who lost their lives in that field near Shanksville. After spending some time at what was then a makeshift memorial at the crash site, we traveled a little farther south into town to visit the chapel.

There was a lovely little garden there surrounding a black granite monument and we spent ten or fifteen minutes in quiet contemplation. As we got back in the car to continue on our journey home, Mom held something out to me and said, "Look what I found."

In the palm of her hand was a monarch butterfly, no longer alive and in pretty ragged condition. We took a moment to look it over and noticed a small, round white sticker on one of its wings. The sticker was no bigger around than the end of a pencil eraser, but it had some writing on it. I squinted to see what it said.

It listed a website, monarchwatch.org, a phone number and a set of three letters and

three numbers, indicating that this was a unique identification tag. We set it on the dash of the car as we left town, and I made a mental note to check it out when we got home.

Monarch Watch, I soon found out, was a research organization out of the University of Kansas that studies the monarch butterfly, concentrating specifically on its migration. By providing special tags to affix to the wings of migrating monarchs and collecting data from those people who may find them, scientists can learn valuable information about their journey.

I reported the find and spent some time exploring the website, with its vast information about the monarch butterfly. It was here where I first learned in detail about the great migration story. No doubt it had been taught to me at some point in my elementary or high school education, but I either didn't remember much about it or I wasn't particularly interested at the time.

The tag on that little butterfly set me off on a journey of my own – one that would over and over again astound me at the miracle of it, the wonder of nature, the tenacity of living things. Over the next ten years I would continue to add to my knowledge and experience about something that had been going on for centuries, with a part of it still taking place right in my own backyard.

I almost couldn't believe that it had taken nearly 50 years for me to discover and appreciate the monarch butterfly. And it took another ten years to find out where that tagged Pennsylvania monarch had started its journey. It had a pretty incredible story of its own, which I'll tell you about later in the book. 🦋

*A turn of events may seem very small
at the time it's happening,
but you never really know, do you?
How can you?*

~ Tom Xavier

# *DANAUS PLEXIPPUS*

The monarch is the most recognized butterfly in North America, some say the world. Its black and orange colors make it one of the most colorful, and its size places it among the largest butterflies occurring naturally in North America.

First noted and named by Swedish taxonomist Carl Linnaeus in 1758, the monarch butterfly enjoys its largest concentration of the world's population in the eastern part of North America. Smaller populations exist west of the Rockies, through Central America into northern South America, in New Zealand and coastal Australia, as well as the islands north of Australia. A few small, isolated colonies have been found in Europe, but are believed to have been introduced via transportation, accidental or otherwise.

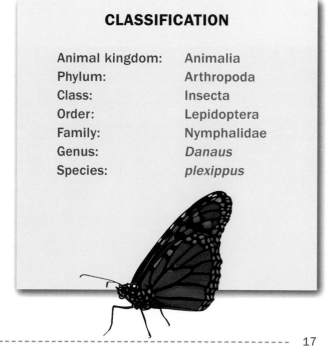

**CLASSIFICATION**

| | |
|---|---|
| **Animal kingdom:** | Animalia |
| **Phylum:** | Arthropoda |
| **Class:** | Insecta |
| **Order:** | Lepidoptera |
| **Family:** | Nymphalidae |
| **Genus:** | *Danaus* |
| **Species:** | *plexippus* |

The monarch's northern range is determined by the presence of milkweed. In North America, the farthest north that milkweed grows is at about 50°N latitude, just north of Winnipeg, Manitoba, in Canada.

It is the eastern North American population that is the most well known, not only for their numbers, but for their epic long-distance migration. For this reason, it garners the most attention when it comes to conservation, though the western population suffers from similar environmental issues.

## Identification

Once you know what to look for, the monarch is quite easy to identify. Its bright orange, black and white coloration is telltale. But not so fast – other butterflies have the same colors and similar markings. In fact, the viceroy is very often mistaken

for the monarch. This comes in handy for the viceroy, as you'll find out later.

The monarch has a wingspan of 3½-4 inches and is marked by several orange cells, bordered by black veining. White spots appear on the outer edges, as well as on the fuzzy black thorax. It has typical butterfly antennae, both of them clubbed on the end.

Males tend to be slightly larger than females and have several identifying marks and features that make telling the sexes apart quite easy. On each of the hind wings, there is a black androconial spot that is thought to play some pheromonal role in mating, but it is not certain just what that role is.

Males also have claspers at the end of their abdomen, which they use to hold on to the female during mating. These are fairly easy to see, if you can get a good look at that part of their body.

While the monarch has six legs, distinguishing it as an insect, only four are clearly visible. The other two legs, called brushfeet, are located beneath the head on the front of the thorax and are carried close to its body most of the time. Brushfooted butterflies belong to the family called Nymphalidae – the largest family in the butterfly order Lepidoptera, with around 6,000 species throughout the world.

Brushfoots include painted ladies, buckeyes, mourning cloaks, emperors, admirals, fritillaries, and others, in addition to monarchs. They're often called four-footed butterflies.

The brushfeet contain spiny hairs all along their length and sharp tarsal claws at the end, which the monarch uses to help identify milkweed. The female will "drum" on the plant's

*Female (top) and male (bottom) monarchs*

surface with them, which releases some of the plant's juices. Chemoreceptors on the legs and feet confirm whether she's on the right plant or not. She probably also has chemoreceptors on her ovipositor, the structure through which she lays her eggs. Since milkweed (and its many species) is the only plant on which their caterpillars feed, distinguishing it from other plants is a very important skill.

The monarch does not grow in size once it has become an adult. Though males are slightly larger than females, some variation in size of the adult butterfly will occur depending on the quality of the milkweed the caterpillar has eaten. Those caterpillars who eat less than some of their friends may form slightly smaller chrysalides and become smaller adult butterflies.

## Life Cycle

A monarch's life begins when a female lays an egg on the leaf of a milkweed plant, usually on the underside, although she can make use of other parts of the plant for this purpose. I've seen eggs on stems and flower buds, but most often it's on the leaves, because those are more tender than the stems – important for the future little caterpillars' jaws. The underside of the leaf also provides some protection from predators and weather.

The female lays her eggs singly; most often, depending on the size of the milkweed plant, she will only lay one egg per plant. She does this most likely to assure that her offspring will have enough to eat without competition from other monarch caterpillars. This also helps avoid cannibalism, because yes, monarch caterpillars will eat other monarch eggs and first-instar caterpillars have been known to eat smaller ones if there's a great discrepancy in their sizes.

 The number of fertilized eggs a single female monarch will lay varies greatly, determined by factors such as weather, availability of milkweed and her age, but is probably somewhere between 400-500.  The largest number of eggs known to be laid by a single monarch is 1,179, by a female raised in captivity. http://monarchlab.org/biology-and-research/biology-and-natural-history/breeding-life-cycle/life-cycle

*Monarch egg*

*Monarch egg next to a grain of salt*

*Monarch caterpillar hatching*

*Monarch caterpillar eating its egg case*

The egg is creamy white in color, and oval with vertical ridges, about the same size as a grain of salt. The egg has a hard outer coating, called the chorion, which helps protect the embryo inside as it develops. An inner waxy lining helps keep the egg from drying out.

The embryo takes about 3-5 days to develop into a very tiny caterpillar, at the end of which time the caterpillar chews its way out of the egg. Next, it turns around to eat its egg casing as its first meal – and for the next two weeks, the caterpillar's one job is to eat milkweed and grow.

Being invertebrates, monarch caterpillars have an exoskeleton that doesn't stretch or grow much, so they must shed it periodically as they outgrow it. This is called molting. Each stage of growth between molts is called an instar, and the monarch experiences five of them.

From the first instar to the fifth, the monarch caterpillar will undergo small changes in its appearance. For example, in the first instar, you won't notice any of the antenna-like appendages called filaments or tentacles that are borne in pairs, one front and one back. The front ones don't appear until the second instar and the back ones don't appear until the third.

The caterpillar has six true legs, which are located on the thorax, near the head. But it also has five sets of prolegs, which are located on its abdomen and help it move around. The prolegs undergo some changes in later instars as well, but these changes aren't quite as noticeable.

At this point, the new outer skin is quite soft and flexible and the caterpillar will take in air, expanding itself as the skin firms up. This, along with the skin's retaining some ability to stretch, allows for some growth throughout that particular instar before the caterpillar has to molt again. The monarch caterpillar, pupa (chrysalis), and adult butterfly breathe through spiracles, which are pairs of openings along the sides of the thorax and abdomen. They take in oxygen and convert it to carbon dioxide, as humans do.

If you've ever raised a monarch caterpillar inside and observed its growth, you know how very quickly it can go from being about 1/16th of an inch in length to just under two inches. You also know how much poop (called frass) all that eating produces!

When the caterpillar molts, it will stop feeding, and will remain still for many hours before beginning the process. The outer skin separates from the inner, with the aid of an enzyme that starts to dissolve the outer skin. The caterpillar will lose its old head capsule first, and the new, lighter-colored one appears. It will then literally walk out of its old skin, and most times will eat it, thus taking advantage of the nutrients it still contains.

During its life as a caterpillar – about two weeks – the monarch will increase in size by 2,000 times, and its weight nearly 3,000 times.

*Frass on milkweed leaves*

*Chrysalis under a fence*

The larval, or caterpillar stage, lasts about 10-14 days. When the caterpillar reaches its fifth and final instar, it will be very plump, its front tentacles quite long, and its colors more vivid than ever.

It is at this point that the caterpillar will start wandering, looking for a suitable location to pupate, or form its chrysalis. Seldom does the caterpillar form its chrysalis on the milkweed plant upon which it was feeding, and it's not uncommon for a monarch to travel 40 feet away to find a place it feels provides adequate protection.

The locations that monarchs choose to pupate can be quite surprising sometimes, and don't always make sense to us. You may see them in a very exposed location, but most often they will be on the underneath side of some surface, where they are less likely to be exposed to weather and predators.

Once the caterpillar has found "the spot," it begins to lay down a circular pad of silk, using its spinneret. Back and forth, round and round, its head goes, until finally it concentrates the silk in one spot near the center. This is called the silk button and it will be what the caterpillar, and eventually the chrysalis, will be suspended from.

Upon completion of the silk button, the caterpillar will walk away and position its rear end over the silk button and grab hold with the anal prolegs at the very end of its body. It will gradually let go with first its true legs, then its remaining prolegs, until it is hanging upside down, in a "J" formation. The caterpillar will hang like this for about 12-16 hours before it sheds its skin for the final time.

When the final molt begins, the caterpillar's dangling filaments will no longer be "perky." They will hang limp and twisted in spirals. Soon the caterpillar will begin contracting; just behind the

*Caterpillar hanging in a "J" formation before starting to shed its skin.*

*Just before the caterpillar molts for the final time, its tentacles will hang limp and twisted.*

head, the skin will split open to reveal the emerald-green chrysalis. Contractions continue, with the old skin proceeding to be split and shoved up, accordion-style, towards the top.

Once the old skin is gathered at the top, a short black post-like structure called the cremaster emerges and begins to embed itself into the silk button. This is a very tenuous and dangerous situation for the monarch. If it falls before the cremaster becomes embedded, the soft chrysalis will not survive.

The cremaster has little hooks on the upper end. The newly revealed chrysalis will writhe and twist in an effort to make sure that the cremaster is firmly attached via these hooks, much like Velcro®. While this is happening, the chrysalis is held secure by two small bumps or tubercles on its surface that hold onto the skin. Once the cremaster is firmly embedded, writhing and twisting continues until the old skin falls off and the chrysalis hangs only by the cremaster.

In the next couple of hours, the new chrysalis will shrink a bit and take on the traditional shape, and will begin to harden. Shiny gold dots will appear in a ring around the top and at other locations.

*During ecdysis, the caterpillar's skin will split behind its head and it will contract over and over as the old skin scrunches up toward the top, accordian style. It will eventually fall off as the caterpillar begins to wriggle and writhe and the cremaster becomes firmly embedded in the silk button.*

**What is the function of the gold dots on a monarch chrysalis?**

Many studies have been done on the gold dots, with no real conclusive evidence as to their function. It has been hypothesized that they may help deter predators, or filter UV light that may be harmful to the monarch, or reflect light from the sun-dappled leaves and enhance the camouflage of the chrysalid.

Over the next 11-15 days, the chrysalis will be home to the developing monarch butterfly. Before it even became a chrysalis, early in the caterpillar's life, imaginal discs within (see Glossary) had already started to develop into the parts of the butterfly. But they were put on hold as the caterpillar ate and grew, until finally, as a chrysalis, enzymes were released, causing the caterpillar body to dissolve into a medium for the discs to once again begin growing and developing into the parts they were meant to be: wings, legs, antennae, all the organs, everything that makes up the beautiful adult monarch butterfly.

As the day of eclosure draws near, the chrysalis will begin to darken and the faint image of wings can be seen. For the next 24 hours or so, it will appear to darken more and more until the butterfly can be seen quite well. The chrysalis itself is translucent, and what has been seen is the monarch reaching the end of its development.

In the final hours, air space develops between the chrysalis and monarch within, and soon a crack appears toward the bottom of the chrysalid (at the top of its thorax), and the butterfly begins to push its way out. As you watch, it seems to be happening in slow motion, but then you realize it actually only takes a few minutes until the adult monarch has freed itself.

Using the tarsal claws on its feet, it hangs on to its chrysalis case (called the cuticle) and begins to pump fluid into its wings. At first, they look like wings in miniature, but soon they will expand and take shape and the swollen belly disappears. The veins in the wing are now filled with hemolymph (blood) but they will require several hours before they're firm enough to fly.

Just after eclosure, you may notice the monarch's proboscis curling and uncurling. It appears to be in two parts, because it is. The monarch works to press the two parts together like a zipper to form the feeding tube through which it will sip nectar. The curling and uncurling of the two parts, along with help from the labial palps nearby, help accomplish this task. You can see the fuzzy palps "clapping"

as they do their work. If the monarch fails to join the two parts of the proboscis, it will not be able to drink and it will eventually starve to death.

Sometimes a newly-eclosed monarch loses its grip and falls. If it is able to walk to something and crawl up to a place where it can hang, the wings will continue expanding normally. If not, the wings may end up distorted and prevent it from flying. A newly-eclosed monarch must hang for the wings to dry properly.

About 3-4 hours later, once the wings have sufficiently firmed up, you'll see the monarch open and close its wings as if to try them out. Eventually, it will take flight and within the next day will seek out nectar for its first meal.

These will be incorporated into the spermatophore, a packet that also contains the sperm, which he will transfer to the female during mating. These nutrients provide nourishment to the fertilized eggs, which increases their chance of survival and the number of healthy eggs that a female will lay.

A female will mate with several males, just as the male will mate with several females. The female will soon begin to look for milkweed upon which to lay her fertilized eggs.

As an adult, summer generations of monarchs will live anywhere from two to six weeks, if they live out their natural life and manage to avoid predators. There will be four or five generations born each year (depending on weather), but the final generation, born in late summer/early fall – the generation that migrates – will live up to seven or eight months.

## Living the life

If the monarch is a male, it will be on the lookout for a female with which to mate. Males are known to be particularly aggressive, pursuing the female until he takes her down. If a successful pairing occurs, he may stay on the ground with her, or will take flight with her attached, and alight in a tree or other plant. They can remain attached for as long as 14 hours.

Prior to mating with a female, the male monarch is known to engage in an activity known as "puddling." He will take up water at the edge of mud puddles or other wet areas, with the purpose of collecting salts and minerals.

### The Methuselah Generation

The final generation of monarchs in late summer and early fall are called the Methuselah generation. Why Methuselah? The name is borrowed from the Bible, in which Methuselah was said to have lived for 969 years, much longer than his contemporaries. Migrating monarchs live five to eight times as long as their parents and grandparents.

# *Did you know?*

Rather than depending on the release of pheromones to attract a female, the male monarch will actively pursue the female in the air, taking her down to the ground. If he is successful in joining with the female, he will hold onto her with his claspers located at the end of his abdomen and fly off with her to a tree or shrub. They can remain connected for several hours.

# THREE

# MONARCH MIMICS

❧

As we stroll through our gardens – or the park or just about anywhere, really – the monarch butterfly grabs our attention. Its striking black and orange coloring often is in strong contrast to its surroundings, yet it complements them beautifully. Knowing that monarchs are not as plentiful as they once were, we count ourselves fortunate to see each and every one.

But is that black and orange butterfly really a monarch we're seeing?

They say that everyone has a twin in the world, and the monarch has its, too. In fact, there are three commonly seen butterflies that can fool you into thinking they're monarchs.

## Viceroy (*Limenitis archippus*)

The viceroy is the butterfly that is the most common victim of mistaken identity. The markings on the monarch and the viceroy are strikingly similar, but they also have distinctive

differences. Once you learn what these are, it's not difficult to determine which one you're seeing.

The viceroy butterfly was once thought to enjoy a certain measure of predator protection solely because of its similar appearance to the monarch (photo on page 31). This type of mimicry (imitation) is called Batesian. However, it has been found that viceroys are distasteful in their own right, classifying them as a Müllerian mimic.

## Queen *(Danaus gilippus)*

The queen butterfly looks very much like the monarch, being the same colors and same general size, but it has different markings on its wings. The monarch has distinctive black veining on its wings, whereas the queen's are more of a solid color with scattered white dots, although when the wings are folded together over their bodies, the veining is much more similar on the ventral (underneath) side.

Distinguishing between the two is more a problem in the South, because the queen's range is generally in the southwestern U.S. and Florida.

Viewing them side by side, it's easy to see both their similarities and their differences. It's almost like those picture games where you're supposed to find the differences between two things. For example, you might notice that the viceroy has a distinguishing black band across the center of its hind wings.

But it's not often that you'll have the benefit of seeing them together in the wild, so consider these other differences: The monarch is noticeably larger than the viceroy. As adults, both species have very little variation in their respective sizes (the monarch always being larger, the viceroy always being smaller), so there's not much chance of seeing a smaller monarch or larger viceroy than usual.

Their flight habits are different too. The larger monarch has extremely graceful, soaring movements. When moving short distances from flower to flower as they nectar, they can flutter quickly, but in flight, they're very elegant. The viceroy has a quicker, more erratic flight.

## Soldier *(Danaus eresimus)*

A lesser-known and -seen cousin of the monarch is the soldier. Found in southern Texas and southern Florida, the soldier bears the familiar orange, black and white coloring of the other mimics, though the black veining is less prominent. Its larvae are yellow, black and white striped, with three sets of tentacles or filaments. The chrysalis is nearly identical to that of the monarch.

# Caterpillar Copycats

Not only are there adult butterflies that can fool you, there are caterpillars that have tripped up many a person with how similar they look to the monarch. You might think the caterpillar forms of these mimics would be the same species as the adult butterfly culprits, but Mother Nature can be a tease.

While the adult viceroy butterfly is most commonly mistaken for the monarch, the viceroy's caterpillar looks nothing like it.

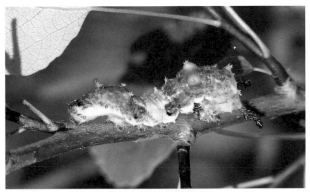
*Viceroy caterpillar*

*Monarch caterpillar*

## Eastern Black Swallowtail

One that does look very similar to the monarch caterpillar is that of the Eastern black swallowtail *(Papilio polyxenes)*. There's no confusing the adult butterflies, yet in caterpillar form, it happens all the time. They're basically the same size, similar colors, and both have stripes. But there are distinctive differences.

The monarch has black, yellow, and white stripes encircling its body, with black tentacles on both front and rear.

The Eastern black swallowtail caterpillar also has stripes, but they're black over light green, with yellow spots interspersed on the black stripes.

*Eastern black swallowtail caterpillar*

The Eastern black swallowtail has another telltale difference: It has an osmeterium, an orange-colored, forked, tongue-like structure that it extends when it's disturbed. It emits a malodorous chemical designed to repel predators, and I find the smell rather offensive myself.

## Queen

If you live within the range of the queen *(Danaus gilippus)* butterfly, their larvae look similar to the monarch's, too, with noted differences being that they have three sets of tentacles, instead of just two, and where the tentacles join the body, you'll notice a reddish color.

*Eastern black swallowtail caterpillar*

*Queen caterpillar*

When seen side by side, it's easy to tell the difference, but perhaps the best determining factor is in where you find them. Monarch caterpillars will always be found feeding on milkweed plants. It's their only host plant. Eastern black swallowtails, on the other hand, will be the ones that are chowing down on your dill, parsley, Queen Anne's lace, rue, fennel or carrots.

# FOUR

# THE MIRACULOUS MIGRATION

**Prior to 1975,** the exact winter location of the migrating monarchs was not known. Yes, they went south, into Mexico, but just where? Dr. Fred Urquhart, a zoologist from Toronto, Canada, along with his wife, Norah, devoted many years to attempting to find this out. Dr. Urquhart developed a system of applying paper tags to the monarchs' wings, each with a unique identification number, tagging his first monarch in 1937. Several hundred thousand tags later, on January 9, 1975, naturalists Ken Brugger and Catalina Trail, with Dr. Urquhart's guidance, found the monarchs clustered in the oyamel fir forests in the Transvolcanic Belt mountains of central Mexico. The discovery of the monarchs' overwintering location was shared with the world the following year, in the August 1976 issue of National Geographic.

**mi · gra · tion**
noun

: The seasonal movement of a complete population of animals from one area to another.

Migration is usually a response to changes in temperature, food supply, day length, and is often undertaken for the purpose of breeding. *(American Heritage Science Dictionary)*

The monarch's migration is extraordinary; there is none like it in the butterfly world. Think of it: A butterfly born in Canada or the U.S. begins an epic journey of up to 2800 miles south to a place they've never been before – a very specific place, where

*When they take flight in the fall, do they know how very far their journey will eventually take them? Or are they simply answering a call within themselves to persevere until they reach the perfect spot that will shelter them for the winter? Do they already know that next spring they will partially retrace their flight northward?*

their great-great-grandparents went the year before, but never the other generations between them.

So much is still unknown about how monarchs make their epic journey each fall. They continue to be the subject of much study by many who desire to learn exactly how they do it. What is currently known is that migration is triggered internally by external cues. Before we discuss what those external cues are, it's important to know that the final generation of the year – the monarchs that will migrate – do not emerge from their chrysalides as sexually mature butterflies. They are in a state of reproductive diapause, which is a temporary suspension of their sexual development.

By not mating until spring, the migrating monarch's energies are instead put toward development of flight muscles and storing lipids within their body for both the long journey and for surviving the winter. Lack of or low levels of the hormone that stimulates reproductive behavior at this point in their development extends their life by months beyond that of the summer's previous generations (that did reproduce).

Adult monarchs that migrate have been shown to have wings that are slightly larger than those butterflies that only live 2-6 weeks and do not migrate. The forewings, especially, may also appear to be darker, indicating that the scales are more densely positioned on them. Both of these factors assist the migrating monarch in its long journey.

This late generation of monarchs emerges from the chrysalis concentrating their efforts on heading south and finding nectar along the way. They will remain in diapause until spring, when they will once again continue with their life cycle as sexually mature adults. It is not until then that they will mate and start back north in search of milkweed, on which the female will lay her eggs.

## Timing is everything

In the fall, the wheels of migration have already been set in motion before the adult monarch emerges from its chrysalis. Even while it was still in its latter stages as a caterpillar, it was already being determined whether or not it would be emerging as a migrating butterfly.

When the angle of the sun reaches 57° off the horizon, the monarch knows that migration is to commence. Simultaneously, the days are also gradually becoming shorter. It's not enough that the days get short; they steadily keep getting shorter. This variation is important. Consecutive days of the same short length will not trigger migration;

ever-shortening day length seems to be the most important determining factor for migration to begin.

## Did you know?

Migrating monarchs expend a lot of energy during the long trip. Unless feeding along the journey has been interrupted or curtailed, monarchs will arrive in Mexico weighing more than they did when their journey began. This is because they take advantage of nectaring as often as possible along the way and because their bodies store energy in the form of fat that will sustain them through the long winter.

In addition to increasingly shorter day length, natural seasonal changes are occurring. While daytime temperatures may remain warm, the nights are becoming relatively cooler. Because of these weather changes, the quality of the milkweed declines. These things work together to signal that it's time to head south. (http://monarchjointventure.org/monarch-biology/monarch-migration)

Migration begins in the farthest north part of their range, in the southern part of Canada, starting about mid-August. Moving in a southern and southwesterly direction, the majority of the monarchs travel through the heart of the eastern part of the U.S.

Monarchs don't purposely gather together in a flock the way birds do. Yet, as they begin to make their way south, they are often seen in both small and large groups, resting for the night or during inclement weather in trees and shrubs.

 A group of butterflies goes by several names. "Kaleidoscope" is my favorite, but others have used the terms "swarm" and "rabble." Take your pick.

It's not known whether they find each other in the air, or whether they join together as they seek the same favorable roosting locations. But as they move farther and farther south, and eventually funnel through Texas, these groups inevitably join up with each other to form ever larger swarms.

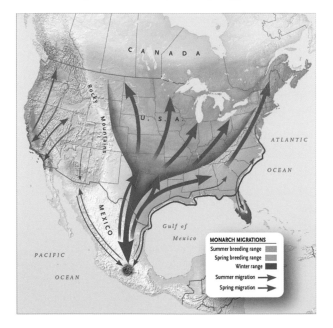

## Migration Roosts

One drizzly cool day in September 2014, my cell phone rang. I looked at the number and recognized it as that of the newspaper for which I write a weekly gardening column. I swiped across the screen and listened as my editor asked, "What are you doing right now? Someone called in, reporting hundreds of butterflies in their trees. Can you run over there and snap a photo for the paper?"

Though it was a mere three miles from my house, I would have driven much farther to see what I knew was an overnight roost by monarch butterflies on their migration journey to Mexico. The call came in the early afternoon and I knew that on a normal sunny day those butterflies would have left those trees hours before.

 All butterflies are cold-blooded creatures, and as such are dependent on the environment to provide heat to them. Monarchs are unable to fly if their core body temperature reaches an average of 55° F or below. On a sunny day, they can bask in the sun, with the scales on their wings absorbing heat and reflecting it back into the black thorax. They are able to fly at 50° F, but on cloudy days, most will not be able to fly when the temperature is below 60° F.

Luckily for me (if not for the monarchs), the temperature had not risen much that day and hovered around 55° F. The misty rain, coupled with that low temperature kept the monarchs parked in those trees, as they cannot fly when their bodies are that cold.

As monarchs travel, they will gather nectar along the way. Night temperatures in the north often fall below the threshold of flying, so they will stop and seek the protection of trees and other vegetation. In the morning, as the sun comes up and warms them and the air around them, they will continue on their journey.

The conditions on the property where I viewed this overnight roost were ideal, with several large willow and pine trees surrounding a small pond. Standing there viewing this natural spectacle, I was overcome with emotion at the wonder of it – all those tiny creatures, so intent on flying ever-southward, no doubt to encounter obstacles they couldn't foresee, until they reached their destination thousands of miles away.

Because of the tagging program, we now know that monarchs that begin their journey closer to the East Coast are less likely to make it all the way to Mexico. They tend to travel in a southerly direction, taking a westerly turn when they reach the Gulf of Mexico. Some will attempt to cross the water there, but it is thought to be impossible for monarchs to successfully cross the Gulf; it is too far and they can't fly at night. Others will follow around the Gulf's northern shoreline on their journey. Still others will keep traveling south to the lower part of Florida, where they will stay for the winter. A small number will continue on to Cuba.

A monarch's antennae have internal circadian clocks that help orient them in the proper direction at the proper time for migration. If a migrating monarch were to lose its antennae, it would likely not be able to find its way and would travel in a random direction.

Those that take the traditional route, using the flyway through the heartland, will funnel through Texas and on to their safe place in the mountains of central Mexico.

## What makes this spot so special?

Though a small number of monarchs spend their winters in other locations, such as southern Florida, where some of them live year round, the majority of the eastern population clearly prefers the conditions that are unique to the Transvolcanic Belt , which extends across Mexico's midsection.

The various monarch preserves are located 60 miles west of Mexico City in high forests of oyamel firs (*Abies religioso*), which only grow at altitudes between 6,900-13,500 feet.

At this altitude, temperatures are cool enough in the winter to slow the monarch's metabolism, helping to reduce their use of fat stores. It can become cold enough to snow, and though the monarchs can survive temperatures as low as 17° F, they won't for long, and especially if they're wet.

When a monarch's body temperature drops into the 30s or 40s, it shivers like humans do, to try to warm itself up to flight threshold.

*The trees are literally dripping with monarchs, and though each one weighs approximately .5 to1 gram, the branches sag from their added weight.*

The fir trees are situated so that they form a canopy, which provides protection to the monarchs from weather that might otherwise be a threat. It protects them from strong winds, driving rains and the occasional snow storm. Temperatures inside the forest are considerably warmer where the canopy is intact. An equally important protection for the monarchs in the oyamel fir forests is the humidity level there – ideal for keeping the monarch from drying out, yet not too wet to foster disease.

With approximately 12 monarch sanctuaries situated on scattered isolated mountaintops, the quality of the forests becomes a very important factor in the success of the monarchs' survival. Any thinning of the density of growth changes the habitat, and that's an issue we'll take a look at a little later.

A visit to the sanctuaries while the monarchs are there will show that they cluster on not only the branches of the fir trees, but also on the trunks. The trees hold warmth within themselves, helping to maintain the body temperature of the butterflies.

On sunny days, they may flutter and come down from the trees to nectar or drink water, but for the most part, they will remain on the trees until the spring weather begins to warm and days become longer.

✿

## Did you know?

Recent studies of Western populations of migrating monarchs by the University of California have shown that a monarch's place of origin can be determined by wing size and shape. The slight differences in shape, structure and hydrogen isotopes in their wings can indicate levels of precipitation and how far the monarchs have traveled during migration.

## The "Day of the Dead" Festival in Mexico

Many species in the animal kingdom keep a consistent migration calendar, and so does the monarch. It reaches its overwintering location in Mexico at approximately the same date each year. They begin arriving on or around November 1st, which coincides with *Día de los Muertos*, or Day of the Dead, a Mexican national holiday, officially observed on November 2nd.

Day of the Dead has been celebrated by the indigenous peoples of the land that includes today's Mexico since around 1800 B.C. It is a time of families gathering together to remember loved ones who have died. Because of the arrival of the *monarcas* (Spanish for monarchs) during this special time, many people believe that these butterflies are the souls of their loved ones coming back to pay them a visit. They often call the monarchs *palomas* (doves) when referring to the souls of children.

In their homes, they construct *ofrendas* (altars of offering) and decorate them with candles, flowers (typically Mexican marigolds called *cempasúchitl*), photos, sugar skulls – and often include toys and trinkets that once belonged to their departed family members. Favorite foods and drinks and a special bread called pan de muerto are set out, but these refreshments are not for the living, and will not be consumed.

On *Dia de los Muertos*, it is said, the gates of heaven open at midnight on October 31st and the spirits of the children who have died come down to reunite with their families for 24 hours. Then, on November 2nd, the souls of the departed adults join them. The celebrations continue at the gravesites, which are also decorated.

In spite of the somewhat sad name, Day of the Dead festivals are happy occasions, a time for families to celebrate the lives of those they have lost and remember them with love. 🦋

# LAYING OUT THE CHALLENGES

❧

**T**here has been a **90% decline** in the monarch population over the last 20 years. A drop in numbers as severe as that begs for some explanation as to why. Has there been some environmental change that makes the monarch's world more hostile to it? And if so, what has happened? Is it something that is naturally occurring or is it something that we as humans have done?

The answer is both.

## Climate change

There's no doubt that our climate is changing. Often we talk about the weather extremes that we have been experiencing in recent years – flooding, tornadoes, hurricanes, winter storms, drought.

It isn't that we haven't always experienced these things, but now we are experiencing more of them, they're more severe, and they're less predictable.

When the monarchs depart Mexico and head northward in the spring, they have one purpose in mind: They've emerged from their state of reproductive diapause, mated, and are in search of milkweed upon which to lay their eggs. They will find it first in Texas.

But Texas has been experiencing droughts for some time now and milkweed generally doesn't do well under those conditions. So the already-weary, seven- to eight-month-old monarchs must push on until they find milkweed that can sustain hungry caterpillars.

Droughts also affect the quantity and quality of milkweed and nectaring plants throughout their spring and summer breeding range farther north. A number of nectar plants are drought tolerant, but monarchs are host-specific insects whose eggs can only be laid on milkweed, so drought is a bigger issue for the milkweed.

Meanwhile, back in Mexico, while monarchs seek shelter in the oyamel fir forests in winter, severe winter storms are occurring with more frequency. It isn't enough that the low temperatures, combined with the moisture, are hazardous to the monarchs, but some of these storms are severe enough that they take down a number of the trees that provide that safe canopy of protection.

The oyamel firs also require very specific conditions in order to thrive, much as the monarchs do, and there are signs that climate

change will affect the health of the trees. As these changes expose the trees to drought conditions and higher temperatures than they are used to, the trees become more susceptible to insect and disease pressures.

These are things that we have little control over, and if those were the only problems the monarchs encountered, their populations would likely be great enough to survive natural occurrences such as drought, the occasional winter storm and natural predators. However, a number of things are contributing to their serious decline for which human actions are directly responsible.

## The human factor

Human beings can be a pretty short-sighted and selfish lot, and that's not meant to be particularly critical, but to motivate us all to be a little more introspective about what we have the ability to change for the greater good.

For example, I really love our yard with its large areas of grass. In my part of the country, we get sufficient rain to maintain a lawn, save for a few

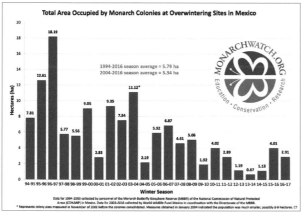

*In winter 2016-2017 the overwintering population dropped 27%, compared to the year before – thought to be partly due to the devastating winter storm that swept through the sanctuaries as they were leaving to return north.*

hot and dry weeks in summer. But for me, a lawn doesn't have to be pristine, in fact, I am quite all right with a lawn containing clover and some dandelions, because I know how valuable those are to pollinators.

Yet, weed-free, lush green carpets can be seen everywhere. They're beautiful, to be sure, but we know what it takes to have that picture-perfect lawn – and if we're all honest about it, we know those chemicals can't be good for a great number of living things, including us.

Pollinators in general are up against some pretty tough odds. We know how important they are to our food supply and the ecosystem in general. I believe that the natural things in our world work in synergistic ways with other natural things, and that we need to consider our actions and what effect they might have on others in this intricately connected ecosystem we live in.

## Pesticides

First of all, we need to define what a pesticide is. You'll see this term used at times in a context that might make you think, "Don't they mean herbicide?" The Food and Agriculture Organization (FAO) of the United Nations defines "pesticide" as:

> "...any substance or mixture of substances intended for preventing, destroying or controlling any pest, including vectors of human or animal disease, unwanted species of plants or animals causing harm during or otherwise interfering with the production, processing, storage, transport, or marketing of food, agricultural commodities, wood and wood products or animal feedstuffs, or which may be administered to animals for the control of insects, arachnids or other pests in or on their bodies. The term includes substances intended for use as a plant growth regulator, defoliant, desiccant, or agent for thinning fruit or preventing the premature fall of fruit, and substances applied to crops either before or after harvest to protect the commodity from deterioration during storage and transport."

WHEW! That's pretty much all-inclusive, so for the most part I'll be using the term pesticide to refer to any chemical means of controlling plants, animals or insects.

In 1996, we saw the advent of Roundup-ready agricultural crops. Roundup® is a pesticide (specifically, an herbicide) that is used to rid farm fields of unwanted weeds. These genetically engineered crops (often called GMOs) were designed to be unaffected by Roundup's active ingredient, glyphosate, making it easier for farmers to treat their fields and raise cleaner and thus more productive crops. One of the so-called weeds was milkweed, which prior to the use of Roundup-ready crops was plentiful and found in many fields.

The monarch's habitat began to quickly disappear from locations where it once grew abundantly.

Do we see a correlation between the introduction of the first genetically engineered crops and the decline in the monarch population?

Though it was never the intent of the makers of glyphosate products to do something that would so profoundly affect the monarch butterfly, among other pollinators, affect them it did. If you take away a large portion of a population's only food source for their young, their numbers will decline. Less milkweed, fewer monarchs.

It would be easy to just place the blame of the monarch's decline entirely on agricultural pesticide use, and it's indisputable that it has had a profound effect on them. On the other hand, you can hardly fault the agricultural community for their desire to raise more productive crops more efficiently. This is just one part of the issue, albeit a large one. Surely, compromise must be possible.

# Did you know?

Most scientists agree that monarch migration began nearly 2 million years ago. The glacial periods caused the milkweed range to move southward and of course the monarchs followed the food source for raising their young. As the climate warmed and glaciers began retreating northward about 10,000 years ago, the milkweed range began inching northward as well. The monarchs chased the milkweed, spring and fall, and the long-range migration we know today was born.

## Chemicals in the garden

Home gardeners have at their disposal some pretty powerful pesticides too. It's all too easy to look at holes in leaves or other plant damage and reach for a spray that will kill whatever is doing the damage. But biodiversity in the garden is a valuable thing and it often involves insects or animals that we as humans may not like. Often, we know deep down that a healthy ecosystem relies on that biodiversity and when we interrupt it with pesticides, there might be a price to pay, however unintended.

## Urbanization and land management

My grandpa, who was a farmer, used to say, "Hold on to the farm. They aren't making any more land." He was right, but the world is growing in population and more people need more places to live. As businesses grow, they often need real estate to expand operations. As infrastructure is updated to keep up with our mobility, areas that were once native and natural are disturbed and reduced in size.

Urbanization happens as a necessary part of a country's economic and physical growth, but it takes its toll on nature. Habitats are made smaller or disappear altogether, and this too has contributed to the monarch's decline.

Even the conversion of CRP (Conservation Reserve Program) land – land that is set aside for conservation purposes – to land that is now used for the production of biofuels has taken away valuable habitat. Fence rows, which were once between farm fields and contained grasses and oftentimes milkweed, are disappearing too, as fields are farmed edge-to-edge.

Milkweed can often be seen growing along roadsides, but indiscriminate mowing is responsible for not only reducing that monarch habitat, but destroying eggs and developing caterpillars each time mowing occurs.

## Western population woes

West of the Rockies, loss of host plant habitat is also an issue, but loss of acreage at the overwintering sites is too. These locations are along the California coast, which is a desirable place for housing developments to spring up, along with the commercial development that goes with it.

As a result of data collected by citizen scientists with The Western Monarch Thanksgiving Count during the overwintering season, there has been an estimated 74% decline in numbers at monarch overwintering locations on the California coast in the last 19 years. (westernmonarchcount.org/about)

It's doubtful that most people have been truly aware of how the reduction in monarch habitat has come about, but as you can see, there isn't a single or simple answer for that. It seems unreal that Monarch Watch estimates the loss of total monarch habitat to be 147 million acres since 1992. That's a lot of habitat. (http://monarchwatch.org/bring-back-the-monarchs/campaign/the-details)

## Illegal logging in Mexico

In 1980, the 56,259 hectares of federal reserve land in the states of Michoacán and Mexico set aside to protect the overwintering habitat of the monarch butterfly was named a Biosphere Reserve. In 2008, the Monarch Butterfly Biosphere Reserve was designated a World Heritage Site by the United Nations Educational, Scientific, and Cultural Organization (UNESCO) meaning that it is legally protected by international treaties.

Despite local protection measures that are in place, and the reduction of land lost each year, the practice of logging, both legal and illegal, remains a problem in the areas surrounding the monarch sanctuaries. In addition, those cleared areas are used for cattle grazing and the growing of food such as avocados.

Those 56,000-plus hectares (just over 139,000 acres) have over 90 owners, including private landowners, *ejidos* (communal land used for agriculture), as well as the government. This puts the forested area and the canopy of insulation it provides at risk and effectively reduces the amount of protection the monarchs have as they cluster in the trees over the winter. It isn't that the landowners don't care about preserving the monarchs, they're simply trying to make a living by cutting and selling the trees.

The monarchs can't seem to catch a break here or there. What's a monarch lover to do? Plenty!

# SIX

# WE CAN LEND A HAND

❧

*M*onarchs, their life cycle and migration are fascinating and incredible. We know they are up against some difficult odds. Difficult, but not impossible. If you're like me, now that you know more about them, you may be inspired to do whatever you can to help them. The ways are many.

Despite of all the publicity and promotion around planting milkweed to save the monarchs, the issue we're experiencing with them isn't that straightforward. It's not really complicated, just multifaceted, and that's a good thing. Realistically, not everyone can do everything, so having several fronts on which to work provides opportunities that may be uniquely suited to one individual or group over another. It's like one body with many parts.

It's encouraging that so many people have rallied around the monarch, and a testament to so many good things. It means that as human beings we're willing to roll up our sleeves and put our best effort forth to right some wrongs, and accept some responsibility for being part of the problem.

One of the wonderful things about life is that we can learn from our mistakes and we very often get second chances. Let's help make sure the monarchs get theirs.

## It's a team effort

Communities and governments are hearing the warning call of the decline of not just the monarchs, but pollinators in general (the honey bee has been a concern for many years now) – and they're all beginning to get help from some mighty sources.

At the annual meeting of the North American Leaders Summit in 2014, President Obama, Mexican President Enrique Peña Nieto and Canadian Prime Minister Stephen Harper addressed the issue of the decline of the monarch butterfly. Out of this meeting came President Obama's 2015 National Strategy to Promote the Health of Honey Bees and Other Pollinators. The goals of the Strategy are to:

* Reduce losses to honey bee colonies during winter to no more than 15% by 2025.

* Increase the eastern population of the monarch butterfly to 225 million butterflies, occupying 6 hectares (15 acres) in the overwintering grounds in Mexico by 2020.

* Restore or enhance 7 million acres of habitat for pollinators by 2020.

While these are lofty and urgent goals, through partnering with a large number of organizations and agencies, the Strategy also provides for long-term planning and implementation of methods to preserve our pollinator species. Continuing research, public awareness and education, increasing and improving habitat, and developing partnerships to achieve the goals are all steps in the right direction.

**Toward increasing habitat:** In February, 2015, the federal government allocated $3.2 million, which is being used in a number of ways. More than 200,000 acres of habitat are being restored across the monarch's range, including establishing school gardens and pollinator gardens. It also has set up a conservation fund dedicated to monarchs that will be made available in the way of grants to landowners who want to conserve habitat.

**Planting more milkweed:** The plan to plant milkweed along the I-35 corridor through the heart of the U.S. – from Duluth, Minn., to Laredo, Texas – is also part of the president's strategic plan. It's an ambitious move, spanning nearly 1,600 miles north to south through the monarch's spring and summer breeding grounds, with the goal of one billion milkweed plants to be grown. Much of it will

be planted by seed and several states have plans in place for collecting wild seed for this use. Monarch Watch has its own campaign for seed collection through its Bring Back the Monarchs initiative.

# Did you know?

Fewer than 5% of monarch eggs and larvae survive to adulthood, due to predators, weather, parasites and diseases.

On another front, in 2016, the USDA's Natural Resources Conservation Service (NRCS) invested $4 million to assist farmers and ranchers in 10 states – Ohio, Indiana, Illinois, Wisconsin, Minnesota, Iowa, Missouri, Kansas, Oklahoma and Texas – in the creation of additional monarch habitat on their property. Participation in the Environmental Quality Incentives Program (EQIP), Wetlands Reserve Program (WRP), and the Conservation Stewardship Program (CSP) fall under this new initiative. Financial assistance to specifically help the monarchs is also available to states outside the targeted area.

## Meanwhile, in Mexico…

There are organizations in Mexico that are working diligently to do what they can to help combat issues in the monarch's overwintering location. With the forests' protective habitat getting smaller in part due to illegal logging, provisions for replenishing the tree growth are being undertaken by several organizations, including Forests for Monarchs, a program of La Cruz Habitat Protection Project, Inc. La Cruz is a U.S.-based non-profit organization that works in the mountain areas of Michoacán, where many of the monarch butterfly reserves are located.

They have been working since 2007 to replenish trees around the remaining habitat, thereby improving the health of the watershed, biodiversity, the forest's microclimate, and combating soil erosion. In addition, efforts are being undertaken with the economic welfare of the local citizens in

mind; by providing them with sustainable forest areas away from the monarch reserves, they can continue to harvest lumber for their local building needs.

In 2016, local police and forestry inspectors were deployed to help monitor the monarch reserves and several illegal logging operations were shut down. They use day and night foot patrols, as well as drones and helicopters to assist them with their efforts.

Even with all that the government and environmental organizations are doing, it will take the combined efforts of not only those entities, but also everyday people like you and me. Most of us don't need a great amount of financial assistance like that to put a plan into place that will make the world more hospitable to monarchs.

## In the Garden

We first look to gardeners as the ones who have the power to make a measurable impact in the recovery of the monarch numbers. Gardeners are literally out in the trenches, and can make the choice as to what they will grow in their gardens and what kind of gardening practices they will use.

We hear the cry, "Grow more milkweed!" and as we know, this is very important. With milkweed being the only source of nutrition for monarch larvae, we must do our best to ensure that there is enough of it in enough locations that it's readily available for the monarchs' use.

Milkweed has the misfortune of having the word "weed" in its name, but it's one of our native wildflowers. I'll never forget the day a few years ago when an older friend, who happened to be a farmer, was walking through my garden and stopped dead in her tracks in front of a small stand of common milkweed. "That's…that's…milkweed!" I smiled and confirmed her observation and explained how important it was to monarch butterflies, knowing that she only saw it as a nuisance in her farm fields.

*Common milkweed*

This is what a lot of us are up against, because we just hadn't typically looked at milkweed in a positive way before we found out how important it is. A change of attitude must take place. Fortunately, we're seeing it happening.

Many of the plants we commonly grow in our gardens today are hybrids of a native plant, bred to keep the most desirable characteristics. That's what we're used to seeing in the majority of garden designs. This practice may have inadvertently demoted our native plants to a lower status.

Native plants often have a freer aesthetic, but they can be integrated into just about any garden design, with attractive results. I'm very much an ornamental gardener and I have a great number of hybrid plants in my garden, but I also grow six kinds of milkweed interspersed among the others and they play quite nicely with their hybrid cousins.

## Milkweed – a plant with a purpose

As the lone source of food for monarch caterpillars, efforts are now being made to purposely plant milkweed where in the past it's been eradicated. Not only does it have beautiful, fragrant blooms, those blooms provide nectar to a number of pollinators besides the monarch.

The U.S., Canada, and Mexico – the three countries that make up the range of the monarch butterfly are home to over 70 native species of milkweed. Several of the species can be found as native habitat over a large part of this area, but others are only found natively in more limited locations.

This doesn't mean that you can't grow a particular type of milkweed that isn't indigenous to your region, but experts do agree that it's preferable to grow mostly those that are. Like any native plant, it will do better if it's grown where it has adapted to the conditions that are unique to a particular area over a long period of time.

According to Monarch Watch, in the U.S. monarchs make use of about 30 different species of milkweed as a food source. At any given location in any given year, they may seem to prefer one type over another. One year it might be common milkweed where you find more eggs and caterpillars, and the next they might be all over the swamp milkweed. This is a good reason to grow several species if you can.

## A Million Pollinator Gardens

If you have a Certified Monarch Waystation, or any pollinator-focused space, you can register your garden with the Million Pollinator Garden Challenge. An initiative begun by the National Pollinator Garden Network, the goal is to increase nectar and pollen opportunities for our pollinators by creating and maintaining at least one million designated pollinator locations across the United States. For more information about how you can participate in this program, visit millionpollinatorgardens.org. And see page 105 for how to create a monarch butterfly waystation.

## In Your Community

Let's just say you're an apartment dweller and you don't own property where you can plant a garden. Maybe you have a patio or balcony; you can certainly grow milkweed and nectar plants in containers. But what if you don't even have that?

Many communities have land set aside for their residents to share. These community gardens are divided into plots that each gardener can use for growing whatever they choose. Most often, these plots are used for growing vegetables, but raising pollinator plants, including milkweed, is a valid option, with a noble environmental cause.

There are also tracts of land such as public parks that usually have flower beds in them. Perhaps you can inquire with their caretakers about the possibility of growing milkweed and late-blooming nectar plants if they aren't already focused on that. Parks for Monarchs, an initiative by the National Recreation and Park Association, has an excellent online guide specifically targeted for park areas, with ideas for how to get the community involved. (nrpa.org/parks4monarchs )

If there is public land available that would lend itself to growing milkweed or nectar plants, maybe you can be the one to contact the proper authorities about the possibility of developing a garden there and volunteer to help with it. Examples? Church property, vacant lots, schools, medians and other rights-of-way, just to name a few.

## Did you know?

**The longest documented migration of a single monarch butterfly:**

*"A tagged male monarch (Danaus plexippus), released by Donald A. Davis (Canada) at Presqu'ile provincial Park near Brighton, Ontario, Canada, on 10 September 1988, was recaptured on 8 April 1989 in Austin, Texas, U.S.A., travelling an estimated 2880 miles, making this the World's Longest Butterfly Migration."*

**Keeper of the Records**
**Guinness World Records, Ltd.**

**Because the butterfly was captured in April the following year, experts believe that this particular butterfly was in the process of making the return trip north, since it could no longer survive the freezing temperatures that Austin experiences in the winter.**

Sometimes just planting a seed in the minds of others by creating awareness is as valuable as taking direct action. Word of mouth has always been a great way to share information, whether it's over your backyard fence, while having lunch with a friend, or via social media.

If you happen to raise monarchs in your house, consider taking it on the road, to schools, nursing homes, or even your place of employment. Who wouldn't enjoy seeing a chrysalis up close and personal? Once you share the life cycle and the incredible migration story, you've most assuredly piqued the interest of those around you.

Kids are especially receptive to hearing about how they can help care for nature, and most of us come

in contact with kids in some way or another, whether it's our own, our grandkids, or the neighbor kids. What about checking with the local library to see if you can read a book about monarchs at story time?

If you keep your eyes open, opportunities will present themselves that will allow you to create awareness or help the monarchs directly. Don't be afraid to step outside your comfort zone if you recognize a chance to take action. Don't assume that someone else will do it.

## A Classroom Helps the Monarchs

Kate Mantenieks' third-grade class at Emerson Elementary in Westerville, Ohio, was studying butterflies. They had planted milkweed in an effort to help the monarchs, when they learned that the city had listed milkweed as a noxious weed. They were faced with the possibility of having to remove the milkweed from their school garden or pay a fine of up to $150.

The science lesson quickly turned into a government lesson, as the students went before the city council to plead their case, asking the council to remove milkweed from their noxious weed list. They explained to the council why milkweed and pollinators were important. In the end, the council voted unanimously to grant their request.

Those students learned a number of valuable lessons under the guidance of their teacher, and their actions were inspiring to those who heard about them. A local newspaper covered the story, which was shared across social media. How many people do you think that third-grade class influenced? The potential is staggering.

# *MexiRocks:*
## Benefiting a Sanctuary Community *and* the Monarchs

The economy is always an issue for the people who live near the monarch sanctuaries in Mexico. Anything that can supplement their income helps deter the illegal logging activities that are destroying the monarch's overwintering habitat there.

Self-proclaimed "Monarch Crusader" Carol Pasternak, of Toronto, Canada, had an idea for creating some income for the local residents. It was an idea that wasn't a handout, but one that called upon their creativity and direct participation. And

"they" were the children of Macheros, one of the local villages near the sanctuaries.

Carol planned a February 2016 trip to visit the sanctuaries. In the months prior, she mulled over her idea and tried it out with a group of friends before presenting it to the children in the school at Macheros. Her idea? Painted rocks.

Now, many of us might scratch our heads at this and wonder how on earth this could work. But even before Carol took her idea to Mexico, she was contacted by Ward Johnson, founder of the Save Our Monarchs Foundation in Minneapolis, Minnesota. He liked her idea and wanted to make the rocks available to sell on his site.

When the time came for Carol's trip to Mexico, she took rocks and the needed supplies to the kids in the school and showed them what they could do. Then she turned them loose with paint and brushes, and what they created were charming, beautiful, one-of-a-kind souvenirs for the tourists and others who might be interested in helping with the financial support of the community.

Named MexiRocks, these artistic renderings of monarch butterfly scenes are now supplementing the incomes of numerous families in Macheros. It doesn't take much, because the cost of living there is comparatively low. With Ward Johnson's help and that of local resident Estela Romero, correspondent for Journey North, the MexiRocks are doing what Carol had dreamed they would.

Carol has made a difference in the monarch community not only financially, but in the pride and satisfaction that those kids feel, knowing they are helping their families while at the same time helping to protect the monarchs.

MexiRocks are available to purchase at the Cerro Pelon Monarch Butterfly Reserve near Macheros, Mexico, and at SaveOurMonarchs.org. The MexiRocks project will be rolled out to other communities over time. Check Carol's website, monarchcrusader.com, for updates.

## Has your city taken the Monarch Mayor's Pledge?

The National Wildlife Federation has a plan. To make it easier for cities to get on board with monarch conservation, the NWF has laid out no less than 24 ways (25 in California) a mayor can lead their city and get citizens involved at various levels. At a minimum, three items on the pledge list must be implemented, but those cities that agree to do eight or more will receive special recognition.

If you've never met your mayor, maybe now would be a good time to introduce yourself and challenge him or her to join the ranks of more than 200 mayors (as of November, 2016) in the U.S. and Canada that have taken the pledge and committed their cities to take action for monarchs. All the details, including documents that can be printed out to help mayors understand the plan and put it into action can be found at the National Wildlife Federation's website: nwf.org/Garden-For-Wildlife/About/National-Initiatives/Mayors-Monarch-Pledge.aspx

## Keep Your Antennae Up!

In April 2016, I read an online news article about a specialized license plate being created in the state of Illinois that would benefit the monarchs. Some of the monies collected from the sales of the license plates would go toward monarch-focused projects and the license plates themselves would create awareness, if nothing else.

I wondered if my state of Ohio had any such license plate, so I went to the Ohio Bureau of Motor Vehicles website to find out. There was a Natural Areas plate, but nothing that would directly benefit the monarchs. It took me about five minutes to decide that I would be the one to initiate the creation of that license plate. Why not me?

The steps were laid out on the BMV site and I got to work. In Ohio, that involved getting a state legislator to introduce a bill providing for the specialized plate's creation, which had to be passed by both House and Senate and then signed by our governor. Once State Representative Tony Burkley started that process, I needed to collect at least 150 signatures on a petition, from Ohio residents who had a registered vehicle in the state, stating that they supported the creation of the license plate.

In addition, I needed to choose an organization that would be the recipient of the designated monies from the license plate sales and obtain an affidavit and logo design from that organization.

I wanted to keep the monies within the state of Ohio, naturally, so I chose Monarch Wings Across Ohio, a division of the national organization Pollinator Partnership. Those who would receive that money in our state were certain city metroparks, arboretums, and others who were working with the organization doing monarch research.

On June 16, 2016, Governor John Kasich signed Senate Bill No. 159 into law, effective September 14, 2016. Once the design was approved and production started, our beautiful monarch license plate made its debut in January 2017. We had done it!

It wasn't that hard. If you're creative in your thinking and keep an open mind about ways that may contribute to the monarch's benefit, you just never know what can happen.

## Be a Citizen Scientist

Many of the programs that scientists and researchers conduct depend on ordinary people to help them collect data. They can't be everywhere, but we are. Those of us who live in the monarch's breeding range – and that's an awful lot of us – have no shortage of opportunities to collect data in such ways as:

* reporting sightings such as first monarch, first egg, overnight roosts, etc.
* counting monarch larvae on milkweed plants
* taking samples of scales from monarch abdomens with tape

* going to coastal overwintering locations and helping with the population count
* tagging migrating monarchs
* monitoring milkweed habitat

For a listing of the many citizen science programs available for all ages and abilities, turn to page 101.

One of my favorite citizen scientist activities is tagging migrating monarchs. In the late summer and fall, I bring in monarch eggs and caterpillars and raise them in my house. As each one reaches the adult butterfly stage, I place an identification tag from Monarch Watch on its hind wing and record the date, location and sex of each one before I release it. When I've released my final one for the season, I submit my data to Monarch Watch.

Each year, I've tagged about 80 monarchs and hope one day that at least one of my monarchs will be recovered, either in Mexico or somewhere along the journey there. It's rewarding for me to be a part of something that will help researchers learn more. You can do this too. See page 119 for How to Tag a Migrating Monarch.

❀

Now let's go into the garden and find out more about the milkweed. The next chapter introduces ten of the most widely found and monarch-friendly milkweeds. And if you turn to page 105, you can find helpful information and plans for creating a monarch butterfly waystation and pollinator garden. 🦋

# WHAT'S SO SPECIAL ABOUT MILKWEED?

*Every* **species of butterfly has specific host plants on which they raise their young.** Many have a number of acceptable host plants, but the monarch utilizes only one group of plants: milkweeds. Part of the reason is that these plants contain a characteristic milky latex sap, giving them their common name.

This sap contains toxic compounds known as cardenolides, which when consumed by the monarch caterpillars renders the caterpillars toxic to some would-be predators. This protection is carried over in the adult butterfly; birds often discover them to be distasteful to the point of making the bird ill. The bird is then conditioned to avoid this brightly-marked butterfly so as to not experience that again!

### Strange but True

Though milkweed provides nourishment for monarch caterpillars, the latex sap inside the plants that helps protect the caterpillars from predators can sometimes spell their death. One study has shown that of the monarch caterpillars that did not survive to adulthood, nearly 30% perished due to the sticky sap gumming up the mandibles of the caterpillar, preventing it from eating. Older caterpillars learn to chew through the large vein of a leaf, effectively stopping the flow of latex to the leaf, thus allowing the caterpillar to eat safely. (http://monarchlab.org/biology-and-research/biology-and-natural-history/breeding-life-cycle/interactions-with-milkweed)

## What kind of milkweed should I grow?

As mentioned previously, it is recommended that gardeners plant milkweeds that are native to their region. But there are a few types that are suitable over a wide area of the monarch's range. Those listed in detail below grow in a large number of states and all are perennial.

*Note:* For an extensive listing of native milkweeds and the regions to which they are native, see the chart on pages xx-xx.

**A Word of Caution:** It should be noted that the latex sap in milkweed (and a number of other plants) can be very irritating to human skin for those who are sensitive or allergic to it. So, until you know if you are one of them, it's wise to use gloves while handling the plants. If you've gotten the sap on your hands or gloves, be sure to keep them away from your eyes! If you do happen to get it in your eyes and experience burning, flush them immediately and thoroughly with water. If the burning persists, get medical care as soon as possible.

**Common Milkweed** *(Asclepias syriaca)*

As the name suggests, this is the plant that most people envision when you mention milkweed. Pollinators of all sorts can be seen visiting these highly fragrant plants when they're in bloom, including honey bees, native bees, flies, beetles, and moths, as well as several types of butterflies. It's a definite favorite of the monarchs.

Its large leaves and relatively tall plants that often form large colonies, bear globes of mauve-colored flowers toward the top of the plant. Once it's established, it spreads not only by seed, but by underground rhizomes. Give this one some room.

Light:          Full sun
Water:          Average
USDA Zone:   3-9
Size:            3-5 feet tall, sometimes taller

Here's a hint to keep it looking good for most of the season: Around mid-season, cut it back by a third, and if you've got a larger stand of it, you can even cut some all the way to the ground. It will grow back rather quickly and the new growth will be better looking and more tender for the monarch caterpillars to eat. Be certain, though, that you inspect what you're cutting to make sure you don't discard monarch eggs or caterpillars. If you do find caterpillars, you can transfer them to another plant.

## Swamp Milkweed (*Asclepias incarnata*)

Swamp milkweed goes by a number of other common names, including marsh milkweed, and rose milkweed. Though its name correctly suggests that it grows in wet locations and is often found growing in wet ditches or river banks, it will survive in places with average moisture too. The flowers are borne in umbels and come in shades of deep pink to white, depending on the variety.

Swamp milkweed can also be spread via underground rhyzomes, but it isn't as aggressive as some, and it tends to stay more coontained. It has smaller, narrower leaves than common milkweed

and takes on a more branched, shrubby appearance than some varieties. Monarchs seem to really like this one if it's available.

Light:          Full sun to part shade
Water:          Average to wet
USDA Zone:   3-6
Size:            3-5 feet tall

Did you know that there is such a thing as milkweed honey? According to those who have tasted it, it's divine and has a wonderful aroma. It takes acres of milkweed in order for bees to make true milkweed honey, so it's a pretty rare commodity, but with the growing of milkweed coming into favor, who knows? Maybe you'll see it around.

### Butterfly Weed (Asclepias tuberosa)

The beautiful orange flowers that have the traditional milkweed shape make butterfly weed a beauty in any garden. It isn't as tall a grower as common or swamp milkweed, but will form a nice thick colony if left alone. Leaves are similar to swamp milkweed, but are much hairier, which may be why monarchs tend to choose other milkweeds over this one.

While this is easily grown from seed, it can take two or three years before it blooms. It has a deep tap root and doesn't take well to transplanting, although it can be done. This one is very slow to emerge in spring, so don't think it's not coming back after its first cold winter in your garden. In spite of all this, it's well worth growing. There is a yellow variety called 'Hello Yellow' that is equally attractive. Note: butterfly weed is not butterfly bush (*Buddleia* sp.), which, however, is a nectar source for monarchs (see page 81 ).

| | |
|---|---|
| Light: | Full sun |
| Water: | Dry to moist, drought tolerant once established |
| USDA Zone: | 3-9 |
| Size: | 1-3 feet tall |

The Perennial Plant Association named butterfly weed *(Asclepias tuberosa)* its Perennial Plant of the Year™ for 2017. Criteria for selection include:

* suitability for a wide range of climatic conditions
* low-maintenance requirements
* relative pest- and disease-resistance
* ready availability in the year of promotion
* multiple seasons of ornamental interest

In addition to those positive qualities, this plant will undoubtedly serve as another ambassador for awareness of the monarch butterfly and the difficulties it's facing.

### Poke Milkweed (Asclepias exaltata)

If you have shady locations, you will want to grow this one. It's one of the few milkweeds that prefer it. It resembles common milkweed and has been known to cross-pollinate with it. Leaves have purplish veining and flowers are sparse, though quite fragrant.

| | |
|---|---|
| Light: | Full shade to part shade |
| Water: | Average to dry |
| USDA Zone: | 4-7 |
| Size: | 2-6 feet tall |

## Purple Milkweed (Asclepias purpurascens)

This milkweed has a very similar appearance to common milkweed, except that the color of the flowers is a much deeper magenta. This has a growth habit much like common milkweed too, spreading by both seed and underground rhizomes, so be sure to give it plenty of room. It too is a favorite of many pollinators, and you'll probably see plenty of monarch activity on this one as well.

Light:        Full sun
Water:        Average to dry
USDA Zone:    3-8
Size:         2-4 feet tall

## Showy Milkweed (Asclepias speciosa)

Showy milkweed is very similar in appearance to common milkweed, though it isn't as aggressive. Its foliage is also hairier. Flowers borne in umbels at the top of the stems range in color from pink to purple. Showy milkweed can be grown in a variety of soil conditions, including those that are somewhat moist, not soggy.

This is a threatened species in Iowa.

Light:        Full sun
Water:        Average to dry, drought tolerant
              once established
USDA Zone:    3-9
Size:         2-4 feet tall, sometimes taller

### White Milkweed (*Asclepias variegata*)

Also called redring milkweed because of the red color encircling the base of its white blooms, its flowers are held in spherical balls at the top of the plant. This one is a real eye catcher that is often found at the woodland edges or in open woods. Locations of full sun may be too harsh for it. It is listed as an endangered species in Connecticut, New York and Pennsylvania.

| | |
|---|---|
| Light: | Part sun to part shade |
| Water: | Average to dry |
| USDA Zone: | 3-9 |
| Size: | 1-4 feet tall |

### Whorled Milkweed (*Asclepias verticillata*)

This is probably my favorite milkweed of all, in appearance and ease of growing. When I point it out in my garden, those who have never seen it before are always surprised that it's a milkweed. It has a feathery, delicate appearance, due to its sliver-like foliage and smaller stature.

The white blooms are tiny as well, and my thought when growing it for the first time was, "How on earth can that support a hungry monarch caterpillar?" While it's true that monarchs could conceivably chow right through it in no time, it spreads well from year to year and the monarchs make use of it in my garden without wiping it out – but that may be because there are also other milkweeds available to them.

It spreads via underground rhizomes, so you might see it come up a little distance from where you've originally planted it. But it's really lovely, so give it a little bit of real estate and let it do its thing.

| | |
|---|---|
| Light: | Full sun |
| Water: | Average to dry, drought tolerant once established |
| USDA Zone: | 3-9 |
| Size: | 2-3 feet tall |

## Green Milkweed *(Asclepias viridis)*

Common names include green antelope horn milkweed and spider milkweed, the latter referencing the crab spider that is often found on it.

| | |
|---|---|
| Light: | Full sun |
| Water: | Average |
| USDA Zone: | 5-9 |
| Size: | 2-3 feet tall |

## Antelope Horns Milkweed *(Asclepias asperula)*

This southwestern native milkweed gets its common name from the seed pods, which tend to curve like antelope horns. Flowers are a creamy yellow-green with maroon-tinged edges.

| | |
|---|---|
| Light: | Full sun |
| Water: | Average |
| USDA Zone: | 7-9 |
| Size: | 1-2 feet tall |

Through its Project Milkweed, the Xerces Society, along with Monarch Joint Venture and the USDA Natural Resources Conservation Service, has created a guide for growing milkweeds that are native to each region. (xerces.org/milkweed).

Two other online sources for information about region-specific native milkweeds:

* Monarch Watch: monarchwatch.org/ bring-back-the-monarchs/milkweed/ milkweed-regions-seed-needs

* The Biota of North American Program (BONAP): bonap.net/NAPA/TaxonMaps/ Genus/County/Asclepias

## Why I left tropical milkweed (*Asclepias curassavica*) off the list

There's no doubt that monarchs love this colorful milkweed, both as a host plant and for nectaring. But it's also been the subject of a bit of controversy, which is why I can't 100% endorse planting it.

Also called scarlet milkweed, blood milkweed and Mexican milkweed, it isn't native to the U.S. or Canada, though it grows fine as an annual in both locations. It's native to Mexico, where it grows as a perennial. It's also a perennial in zones 8b and warmer in the U.S., remaining evergreen in zones 9b-11.

Experts disagree on whether or not tropical milkweed should be grown, especially in areas where it can survive the winter months. In areas where *A. curassavica* can be grown year round, non-migratory monarchs who feed on it were nine times as likely to be infected with the parasite *Ophryocystis elektroscirrha* (OE) as migratory monarchs. (Integr. Comp. Biol. (2016) 56 (2): 343-352. doi: 10.1093/icb/icw030 First published online: June 1, 2016 http://icb.oxfordjournals.org/content/56/2/343)

Still other studies have shown that monarchs that were raised on *A. curassavica*, which has a higher cardenolide toxicity level, had a higher resistance to OE infection (see page 91) and tolerated it better when they were infected. In additional studies, it appeared that infected female monarchs preferred to lay their eggs on the more toxic *A. curassavica* over other species when it was available, perhaps to provide a benefit to their offspring, suggesting that monarchs may have the ability to self-medicate. (See *Monarchs in a Changing World: Biology and Conservation of an Iconic Butterfly* by Karen Oberhauser, Kelly R. Nail, and Sonia Altizer. 2015, Cornell University Press. Chapter 7: p 88-89)

Another concern is that perhaps growing tropical milkweed year round somehow delays the onset of migratory behavior. Again, experts in the field are not in agreement. A combination of things triggers monarchs to emerge in a state of reproductive diapause and then begin migration, with day length being the strongest determinant, followed by steadily cooler night temperatures. The declining quality of milkweed later in the season may also contribute. Studies continue on all these aspects.

## So what's a monarch mama to do?

At this point, it is recommended to always plant native milkweeds when possible, especially those that are native to your region, but I'm hesitant to completely banish milkweed from all gardens everywhere. Monarchs need milkweed, and in some cases tropical milkweed may be an option for providing a host plant when others are in short supply.

Tropical milkweed plants should, however, be cut back in fall and winter months in locations where it grows year round, to decrease the transmission of OE. In colder climates, where *A. curassavica* can only be grown as an annual and frost kills it off, OE is not nearly as prevalent and growing tropical milkweed may not seem to be a problem. And yet, according to Dr. Lincoln Brower, it is indeed a problem, because tropical milkweed is very attractive to monarchs and can interfere with the fall migration when monarchs prefer to stay near this year-round plant and just stop migrating. Dr. Brower advises us to "avoid planting it, period."

# Milkweed Goes to War

During World War II, shortages of many commodities were common. Among them, kapok and rubber. Kapok is a fiber from the kapok tree *(Ceiba pentandra)*, once widely cultivated in Indonesia. The silky fibers were once

used extensively for stuffing, including military life vests and flight jackets, due to its buoyancy and insulating qualities.

When Japan occupied the Dutch East Indies (now Indonesia) during the war, the U.S. supply of kapok was cut off and the military had to examine other similar products to replace it. Milkweed floss was a natural, and the U.S. had lots of it.

Since the regular work force was already either away at war or employed at home, the call was put out to school children in 29 states where milkweed was prevalent. In 1944, Rear Admiral E. L. Cochrane, chief of the Navy Department's Bureau of Ships, made the plea:

*"The Navy needs milkweed floss to replace kapok in life jackets. American boys and girls who want to save the lives of American fighting men, who want to contribute directly to victory, pick milkweed pods."*

In September, when milkweed pods were drying, mesh onion sacks were distributed and the kids got to picking. They were paid a small amount for each sack they collected – usually 15 cents a bag,

with a 5-cent bonus if the pods were dried. In the end, an estimated 11 million pounds or 1½ billion pods were collected, enough to fill 1.2 million life vests.

Methods of extracting the latex sap in milkweed and turning it into rubber were also explored, to counteract the rubber shortage. Unfortunately, it didn't prove to be economically feasible, owing to the relatively low concentration of latex. (washingtonpost.com/wp-srv/special/metro/urban-jungle/pages/120925.html)

## Did you know?

Common invertebrate predators who seemingly aren't affected by the milkweed toxins include stinkbugs, ants, wasps and lacewing larvae.

# Growing Milkweed from Seed

Perennial milkweed seed does have some unique growing requirements, so if you haven't typically had good luck growing it, here are some possible reasons why and what you can do. The seeds require a period of cold moist stratification to germinate. This happens in nature, in colder climates, when the seed drops from the seed pod to the ground in the fall, then goes through winter, with its cold temperatures and moisture in the form of rain or snow. The seed coat is loosened and germination occurs more reliably.

If you live in a climate where you get an extended period of freezing in winter, you can sow the seed in fall through mid-winter. The freeze-thaw cycle with perform its magic and you'll get seedlings in the spring, when temperatures are optimum for growing, according to Mother Nature's schedule. Milkweed is a good candidate for winter sowing in containers too (see wintersown.org for more information on using this method).

Stratification can be mimicked inside when sowing seed in the spring. Simply lay the seeds in a single layer on a wet paper towel, fold it over, then place in a sealed plastic bag and keep in the refrigerator for 4-8 weeks. (Some varieties require longer stratification times than others.) As an alternative to cold stratification, some growers have had germination success by soaking the seed in hot water for 24 hours prior to sowing.

Once the seeds are ready for sowing, press them onto the surface of the soil. Light is required for germination, so don't cover them with any more than a thin layer of soil, if that. Birds and rodents may steal some of the seeds, so oversowing may guarantee a higher seedling success rate. Be sure to keep the seeded area moist, though not overly wet.

# A Milkweed Imposter

Just as there are monarch mimics in the butterfly world, there milkweed mimics in the plant world. Here's one you should know about: **Common dogbane** *(Apocynum cannabinum)*.

Many a gardener and monarch enthusiast has been fooled by this one, so don't feel bad if it happens to you. As you're out hunting for milkweed to feed your monarchs (if you don't happen to have any available in your garden), you may come upon a plant that for all the world looks like milkweed. Except that it isn't. It's dogbane – and monarchs cannot eat it.

Oh, it has very similar leaves to some milkweeds, and it has a somewhat similar growth pattern to a few of them. It even exudes white, milky sap when you break it, which isn't surprising, since it's also a member of the *Apocynaceae* family – same as milkweed. So, how can you determine if it's milkweed or dogbane?

*Dogbane stem (left) and common milkweed stem (right)*

If it's in bloom, you'll be able to see that the flowers don't look like the typical milkweed flowers, but even when it isn't in flower, there's one important difference: If you cut a stem and look at the cross-section, you'll see a solid stem. Milkweed stems are hollow. Stems of dogbane tend to be reddish in color, though not always.

Also known as Indian hemp, dogbane has great pollinator value, especially early in the season, where you'll see plenty of activity when it's in bloom. It's a host plant for the caterpillar of the snowberry clearwing moth, and many species of pollinators make use of it as a nectar source. But monarchs will not lay their eggs on it nor will the caterpillars eat it.

# Nectar Plants are Important Too

There's usually no shortage of nectar-rich plants during the summer, but as the season winds down into fall, they're a little harder to come by. Purposely planting those that bloom later in the summer through frost will provide fuel for the monarchs' journey south, and you'll get to enjoy your garden much longer too. See the nectar plant chart on page 145, which will give you the bloom times for many of the mid- and late-season plants. These annuals and perennials are favorites of the monarch, but you'll see other pollinators loving on them too!

It's also important to grow nectar plants as a food source during the summer reproductive season, as well as late-season bloomers. Since each generation's reproductive success depends on good nutrition, the benefits of having plenty of nectar plants available are many and important. Healthier monarchs just produce healthier offspring and more of them.

Nectar sources remain a priority throughout the monarch's late summer and fall migration, when milkweed may no longer serve a purpose as a food source, unless it's blooming. The migrant monarchs do not mate or lay eggs on their way south, and they rely on good nectar sources to fuel their trip.

The northernmost migrants have a long journey of more than 2,000 miles, and it takes a lot of energy to fly that far. Not only do they need to fuel their flight, they need to store fat in their bodies to sustain them through the winter. Unless starved along the way, they always arrive with huge amounts of fat and weigh more than when they first began their trip.

## What You Should Know Before Planting a Butterfly Bush

Butterfly bush (*Buddleia* sp.) is another plant that raises eyebrows when praise is lavished upon it for its butterfly-attracting qualities. With honey-scented panicles of bloom that are often visited by many species of butterflies – including the monarch – and also a host of other pollinators, what could go wrong?

In this case, it's a matter of location. *Buddleia*, a native of China, is on the invasive species list in Washington, Oregon and Tennessee, where it has been a problem, crowding out native plants and negatively affecting ecosystems. It is also listed as an invasive in Redwood National Park in California. In my Ohio garden, however, it isn't a problem at all. In fact, I count myself lucky if it survives our sometimes brutal winters.

Though there are sterile cultivars available, some of those have been known to revert to the original species, which again becomes a problem in sensitive areas. With so many other plants available that attract butterflies and other pollinators, consideration should be given before planting butterfly bush, depending on your location.

## Think before you spray

Have you heard the phrase, "First, do no harm?" That's a good philosophy to follow in your yard and garden. Many of us want pristine gardens with perfect plants and abundant produce. It's easy to just spray this or sprinkle that, to rid our gardens of those pests that prevent it from looking or performing its best. But pesticides (which includes herbicides) are rarely judicious in their mode of action. For example, you can't apply something meant to kill one kind of pest without its having a detrimental effect on another. Often we feel that using organic products is less harmful, but don't let them give you a sense of false security. Products that are meant to eliminate insects will do just that, organic or not.

## Did you know?

Monarchs can't fly in the rain. They will rest in a shrub or a tree until the rain is over and the water has evaporated from their wings.

A particular group of insecticides called neonicotinoids (neonics, for short) has been recognized to be lethal to honey bees and other insects, including monarchs. Garden centers are now much more aware of the effects of using such chemicals on the plants they sell and the EPA is currently taking another look at these. In many cases, use of a chemical doesn't need to come into direct contact with the insect itself. It's often a systemic version used and it becomes part of the plant material, and then, when the larval form of the insect consumes it, it causes their death.

Many a sad story has been told of well-meaning monarch enthusiasts buying milkweed plants at their local nursery, only to have the heartbreak of seeing their monarch caterpillars die when they've eaten the leaves. It may not have been the nursery that's to blame for applying the pesticide, but rather their supplier. Always ask someone in charge if a particular garden center's plants have been treated with chemicals. If they can't be certain, both at the point of purchase and at the supplier level, it's risky to purchase plants with the intent of feeding them to your monarchs.

No one wants to intentionally hurt honey bees or monarchs, but they are often collateral damage in the use of pesticides; the fewer of these you use in your own garden, the better.

# EIGHT

# PREDATORS AT LARGE

𝔍n spite of the toxic sap in milkweed offering some protection against predators, monarchs fall victim to their fair share. It's all part of the circle of life, I suppose, but when monarch numbers are dwindling, we don't like to think about how those predators interact with them. Here are some of the most common:

## Tachinid Fly

The tachinid fly is perhaps the most well known and bothersome of all monarch predators. Though in the grand scheme of things it's a beneficial insect, it's anything but to the monarch. The tachinid is a common inhabitant of the garden and looks much like the common housefly. Its list of hosts is long: among them are gypsy moths, cabbage loopers, Japanese beetles, armyworms, cutworms, sawflies,

*Parasitized caterpillar with tachnid fly eggs*

I've seen this one in action. One day I was inspecting my milkweed in the garden, looking for monarch eggs and caterpillars. To my dismay, I found a dead caterpillar being eaten by a spined soldier bug. The bug pierces the body of the caterpillar and literally sucks the life out of it.

Stinkbugs have a similar shape and color and are known to be monarch caterpillar predators, too.

codling moths, tent caterpillars, squash bugs – and unfortunately, the monarch.

The adult female parasitizes the monarch caterpillar by laying eggs on its skin. The larvae hatch and burrow into the caterpillar and feed, then pupate inside it. Depending on when it was parasitized, the caterpillar may die before pupating, or it may continue its life cycle through to the chrysalis stage, only to eventually succumb.

Evidence of tachinid fly parasitization can be seen when the fly's larvae or pupae emerge from the caterpillar after its death. As they exit a chrysalis, you may see a thin, white gelatinous strand hanging from it, with the larvae or pupae lying below.

## Spiders

Spiders often lie in
wait in the flowers of
plants, in the hopes
of grabbing a bite to
eat. They can be well
camouflaged, so the
nectaring monarch may
not notice it's there.
Flying monarchs can
also become caught in
spider webs, where they will eventually become that
spider's meal. Spiders are known to eat monarch
eggs and attack the caterpillars.

## Paper wasps *(Polistes* spp.)

Paper wasp nests can usually be found under
overhangs on homes or on the underneath of porch
ceilings and other protected areas. The grayish-
brown papery nests have a honeycomb appearance
and hang from a central stalk. These wasps are
known to prey on caterpillars and are a significant
predator of monarchs, usually attacking medium-
sized caterpillars.

## Trichogramma wasp *(Trichogramma* spp.)

Trichogramma wasps are extremely tiny; a full-
grown one is just 1/50 of an inch in length.
They're considered to be a beneficial insect and
are widely used as a biological control agent. But
they are not a friend to monarchs! They do their
damage as a parasite, by laying eggs in the monarch
egg, effectively killing the developing monarch
caterpillar inside. You know they must be small to
do that.

## Chalcid wasp (many species)

This tiny wasp parasitizes the monarch when it's in chrysalis form. Before the chrysalis has a chance to harden, the chalcid wasp pierces the surface and lays eggs, sometimes hundreds of them. The chalcid larvae kill the developing pupa and eventually exit the chrysalis as adult wasps. Again, the chalcid wasp is considered to be a beneficial insect, just not for the monarch.

## Fire ants (Solenopsis invicta)

Though many kinds of ants can be deadly to monarchs, the fire ant seems to be the most significant. Ants will eat monarch eggs, but they more often will attack the monarch caterpillar by repeated biting until the caterpillar is rendered helpless. They then feast on it.

❧

We should remember that insects are an important part of a healthy ecosystem, and predation and death is a natural part of insect life. Always weigh the benefits versus the disadvantages when deciding to interfere with the natural flow of things.

Note: For a more extensive list of the insects you may find in your milkweed, see *Milkweed, Monarchs and More: A Field Guide to the Invertebrate Community in the Milkweed Patch*, by Rea, Oberhauser, and Quinn. 🐝

# Did you know?

The striped markings on the monarch caterpillar serve as a warning to predators that their bodies contain toxins from its food source, the milkweed plant. In the adult butterfly, the orange and black markings serve the same purpose. This kind of defense strategy, in which the monarch's predators associate their markings with tasting bad so they avoid them, is called aposematism.

# Birds

It's well known that the majority of birds that would normally eat butterflies tend to avoid the monarch, due to the foul-tasting toxin carried in their bodies from the milkweed they ate as a caterpillar. One unfortunate encounter with that and they've learned their lesson. But there are some species of birds who are seemingly unaffected by the toxin and they remain potential predators.

During the summer months spent in North America, the rufous-sided towhee, European starlings and scrub jays all are known to consume monarchs with few or no ill effects.

## Predators in winter

It would be nice to think that once the monarchs start their migration in the fall, fleeing the impending winter weather, they could escape predators, too. Unfortunately, there will be some waiting for them when they get to the fir forests in Mexico.

The toxins from milkweed that have afforded them some protection in the north will continue to play a protective role while they are overwintering. In Mexico, there are 37 insectivorous and omnivorous bird species, and most will leave them alone, but two of them, seemingly not bothered by the toxins, notoriously cause the monarch problems.

Imagine all those thousands of monarchs dripping from the trees – so many of them all conveniently in one spot. It's no wonder that two bird species in particular – the black-backed oriole and the black-headed grosbeak – arrive in numbers to partake of the monarch banquet.

Another Mexican predator works the forest floor at night whenever monarchs come down from the trees: the black-eared mouse (I'm sensing a bleak, black theme here!), which dines on living, dying and recently dead monarchs.

Together, it is estimated that these predators are responsible for 15% of the monarch mortality in the overwintering population.

# *Ophryocystis elektroscirrha*

Every organism on earth is susceptible to disease of some sort or another, and the monarch is no exception. Perhaps their most well-known and studied is *Ophryocystis elektroscirrha*, often abbreviated to OE. (I can't imagine why!)

OE is a protozoan parasite that first infects monarch caterpillars when they ingest the OE spores. Once a caterpillar is infected, it is always infected and as an adult has the potential to pass OE on to other monarch caterpillars.

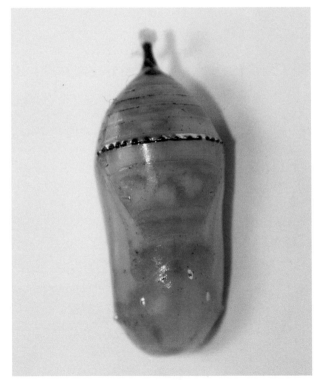

***Chrysalis infected with OE***

In the adult butterfly, the OE spores are carried mainly on the abdomen, and when a female lays an egg on a leaf, some of the spores may be inadvertently scattered over the egg and leaf surface. When the caterpillar hatches from its egg, one of the first things it does is eat its eggshell. If there are OE spores on the eggshell, the caterpillar will become infected. Any spores that are on the surface of the leaf are also at risk of being ingested.

OE can affect a monarch in ways that can shorten its life and change the quality of its life in a negative way. Those that are severely infected may never eclose from their chrysalides, while others will experience such things as wing deformities that interfere with flight. A mild OE infection may result in smaller chrysalides, thus smaller adult butterflies. They may not be able to fly as well. Still other infected monarchs will show no signs of having OE, though they can infect others.

OE is present in all populations of the monarch, but in North America, it is most prevalent (with 70% infected) in southern Florida and Bermuda, where small populations live year-round. The lowest incidence of OE (8% infected) is in the eastern migrating population. 🦋

---

*Sources:*

http://monarchparasites.uga.edu/whatisOE

http://monarchparasites.uga.edu/whatisOE/
Altizer2001.pdf

Monarchs in a Changing World by Oberhauser,
Nail, and Altizer.

# NINE

# ARE MONARCHS IN DANGER OF EXTINCTION – OR NOT?

*This can be a confusing subject for many of us.* Everyone talks about saving the monarchs, even the title of this book is stated this way. But it's probably a simplification of the issue. Without getting too technical, let's have a look at the situation.

The monarchs that make up the eastern North American population – the one that's the subject of the conservation efforts – is classified as *Danaus plexippus*. This particular species also has populations in other parts of the U.S. and the world, though none is as large as this one, nor do they migrate such a long distance. Because of this, the likelihood of *Danaus plexippus* disappearing from the world is not likely. However, the phenomenal migration of the eastern North American population is under threat, if things don't change.

When the study on this subject was published in the journal Scientific Reports in March, 2016, it was predicted that the eastern monarch population had an 11–57% chance of quasi-extinction in the next 20 years. That's not the kind of news we like to read.

The monarch is a tropical butterfly that cannot survive our northern winters. But as numbers dwindle in the breeding grounds throughout summer, fewer will survive the fall migration, overwintering, and the spring migration back into the southern U.S. Those monarchs who do are the ones that provide the population for the following year. As fewer monarchs inhabit the overwintering locations, their survivability decreases, because the probability of mortality – with fewer numbers occupying tinier areas – increases.

## Definition of quasi-extinction

When a particular population of a species declines to a low point, below which recovery is unlikely, we say it has reached quasi-extinction. For example, the monarch population is greatly affected by degradation of the overwintering forests in Mexico and loss of breeding habitat in the U.S. and Canada, pesticide use, climate change, urbanization and disease. Though the monarch has proven to be resilient to some degree, pressure from its threats may be too much for it to rise above if efforts are not made to reduce those threats.

The data for such predictions varies widely due to the difficulty in obtaining exact counts. That

used for this study represented data from 1993-2014 and included overwintering populations, taking into account density of monarchs in those locations, which can be difficult to accurately measure. Data for this part of the study was provided by the World Wildlife Fund-Mexico and the Monarch Butterfly Biosphere Reserve (MBBR).

Also taken under consideration were egg counts from the summer breeding grounds. The counts were conducted by citizen scientists in the U.S. and Canada for the Monarch Larva Monitoring Project (MLMP) as administered by The University of Minnesota. This too, is subject to wide variation. A third component that was considered was an estimate of the amount of milkweed habitat currently present, including the density of milkweed per habitat as well as area occupied by such habitat (data provided by the USDA).

What all this means (given the most generous data and taking into account the average population growth over a period of years) is that if things continue the way they are going now, the eastern population is at risk of reaching a population count too low from which to recover.

## There is reason for optimism

But the good news is that even in the short time that expanded efforts have been taken to conserve the monarch, the increase in habitat has been measurable. For example, in Iowa, which is at the heart of the monarch's summer breeding grounds, more than 112,000 additional acres of farmland were enrolled in the federal government's CRP program for use as pollinator habitat in 2016 alone.

Of course, other factors, such as agricultural herbicide use in North America and deforestation in the monarch's overwintering locations, are significant in influencing the monarch's survival; but restoration of habitat in the monarch's spring and summer breeding grounds in the U.S. and Canada contributes significantly to the effort to bring the monarch's numbers to a level at which it can survive and be with us for many years to come.

# The Endangered Species Act

Many of us can remember in the '70s when America's national symbol, the bald eagle, was endangered. If you take a look at that success story, you'll see that it has some eerily familiar parallels to the monarch situation we have today.

## The return of the bald eagles

So much of the flora and fauna in our world has disappeared over the years, for various reasons. Environmental changes account for the biggest share of those and many of those were a natural progression of things. But human activity has also contributed to the story.

In 1782, the United States adopted the bald eagle as its national symbol. At that time, it is estimated that there were as many as 100,000 nesting eagles. But 100 years later it was a different story. The eagle, as a bird of prey blamed for the deaths of poultry and domestic livestock, was hunted down and numbers dwindled.

By 1940, the bald eagle population had taken such a nosedive that Congress took measures to protect it. They passed the Bald Eagle Protection Act, in which killing, selling, or even being in possession of them was prohibited. In 1962, the act was amended to include the golden eagle.

Shortly after, due to the discovery by Swiss chemist Paul Müller in 1939 that the chemical DDT had insecticidal properties, DDT use exploded as an agricultural insecticide. So hailed

was this discovery that Müller was awarded the Nobel Prize for it in 1948.

The increase in DDT use resulted in chemical runoff that made its way to rivers and streams, and eventually to fish and other animals that frequent such locations. Bald eagles, among other birds and animals, suffered collateral damage. Ingestion of fish – the bald eagle's main food source – that was tainted with DDT caused such thin shells that the eagles' eggs broke during incubation; some failed to hatch at all. Their numbers took yet another tumble.

By 1963, there were only an estimated 487 nesting pairs of bald eagles. Something had to be done. In 1967, bald eagles south of the 40th parallel were protected by the Endangered Species Preservation Act of 1966.

## Definitions, please!

There is often confusion whenever a species is said to be *threatened* or *endangered*. The two terms have distinct but related meanings. According to the U.S. Fish & Wildlife Service, under The Federal Endangered Species Act of 1973, they are defined as:

**Threatened** – any species that is likely to become an endangered species within the foreseeable future throughout all or a significant portion of its range.

**Endangered** – any species that is in danger of extinction throughout all or a significant portion of its range.

Due in part to the 1962 publication of Rachel Carson's *Silent Spring*, a book that brought to light the harmful effects of indiscriminate pesticide use, the Environmental Protection Agency took action that led to the 1972 ban of DDT use in the United States.

The Endangered Species Act of 1973 provided for the U.S. Fish & Wildlife Service to list the bald eagle as endangered in all lower 48 states except for Michigan, Minnesota, Oregon, Washington and Wisconsin, beginning in 1978. (In these states, it was listed as threatened.)

The endangered listing allowed for captive breeding programs and reintroduction efforts, enforcing the law under the Endangered Species Act, as well as providing some protection of nesting sites during breeding season.

A great degree of success came from these efforts and in July 1995, the status of the bald eagle was changed to threatened. Since then, through further evaluation and public input, the bald eagle was found to have made such a recovery as to be removed from the threatened and endangered species list altogether. It is, however, still protected by the Migratory Bird Treaty Act and the original Bald and Golden Eagle Protection Act, and as such, killing, selling or harming eagles, their nests or their eggs is prohibited.

## What about the monarch?

In light of the hard place the monarch is in right now, it might seem that the thing to do would be to place the monarch on at least the threatened species list. In fact, a petition to do just that was filed in August of 2014, through the combined efforts of The Center for Biological Diversity, Center for Food Safety, Xerces Society and monarch scientist Prof. Lincoln Brower.

In December of that year, the U.S. Fish and Wildlife Service determined that the species may warrant protection, leading to an official review that was to be acted on in 12 months. When by March of 2016 the Service still had not acted, a lawsuit was filed and a legal settlement was reached, in which a decision must be made by June, 2019.

There are those who are opposed to the monarch being placed on the list, feeling it is unnecessary or premature, for reasons that I will not detail here. To mention one concern, interaction with any species that is placed on this list will be regulated. In addition, some of the actions required in an attempt to bolster the populations as outlined under the petition, are already being done.

In 2015, President Obama took steps to address the issue of pollinator decline by forming a task force charged with developing a plan to improve the situation on several fronts. The resulting 64-page plan – *National Strategy to Promote the Health of Honey Bees and Other Pollinators* – lays out steps to benefit monarchs specifically.

Currently, many state governments and organizations are responding by taking measures to positively combat the issues that monarchs are up against, namely increasing their habitat. It seems that every week we read of a new initiative designed to do just that.

Whether or not placing the monarch butterfly on the threatened or endangered species list will be in the best interest of the monarch and those of us who enjoy them in various ways is not something I'm willing to take a definitive stand on. It is in the

hands of persons much more knowledgeable about the situation than I am.

I'm thankful that the importance of conserving the monarch is being seen as a priority and that people care enough to want to be proactive in halting its decline and increasing its numbers before it's too late.

Please keep in mind that this is a very current issue, and as such it is a fluid one. At the time of this writing, the information presented here is accurate, but by the publication date of this book, it very well may have changed or been acted upon.

For the most up-to-date information on the decision to place the monarch on the threatened or endangered species list, see the Center for Biological Diversity's site at biologicaldiversity.org/species/invertebrates/monarch_butterfly.

# Ways to Help the Monarch:

*Projects for Everyone*

# *Citizen Science Programs*

There are numerous opportunities for us to be citizen scientists. The list here is by no means exhaustive, but these should keep you busy.

### Project Monarch Health – monarchparasites.org

This program from the University of Georgia enlists the help of citizens who take samples from monarchs in the wild and provide them to scientists who study the spread of a protozoan parasite across North America.

### Monarch Larva Monitoring Project – mlmp.org

The Monarch Larva Monitoring Project (MLMP) is a research project administered by the University of Minnesota. Using data collected by citizen scientists in the U.S. and Canada, they seek a better understanding of how and why monarch populations vary during the spring and summer breeding seasons in North America.

### Monarch Watch Tagging Program – monarchwatch.org

Citizen scientists help with the monitoring of the monarch migration by tagging the migrating generation of monarchs found or raised from locations throughout the U.S. and Canada.

Participants submit their tagging data to Monarch Watch, which administers the program through the University of Kansas.

### Journey North – learner.org/jnorth/monarch

Citizen scientists report sightings of monarch eggs, larvae and adult monarchs, as well as overnight roosts. There are opportunities for reporting data for other wildlife species here too.

## Citizen Science Opportunities for the Western Monarch Population

### Southwest Monarch Study – swmonarchs.org

The Southwest Monarch Study, based in Phoenix, studies the migration and breeding patterns of monarchs in the southwestern U.S. (Arizona, Nevada, New Mexico, California deserts, Utah and western Colorado) through their tagging program. They also monitor milkweed habitat.

### Western Monarch Thanksgiving Count – westernmonarchcount.org

Every year, for three weeks around the Thanksgiving holiday, citizen science volunteers go to the 100+ overwintering sites on the California coast to take a count of the monarchs that are utilizing those sites.

### Monarch Alert – monarchalert.calpoly.edu

Administered through Cal Poly, San Luis Obispo, this tagging program depends heavily on citizen scientists and focuses on studying the demography and population fluctuations of the Western population of the monarch butterflies.

### Monarch Citizen Science – pgmuseum.org/monarch-citizen-science

The Pacific Grove Museum of Natural History in Pacific Grove, California, provides the opportunity for middle school, high school and college students, and adults, to collect data at the monarch overwintering sites in Monterey County. They also conduct year-round habitat monitoring. Other volunteer opportunities exist, such as being a monarch docent and event assistant.

And speaking of science…

# Monarchs in Space

On November 16, 2009, three monarch caterpillars in their 4th instar accompanied the astronauts of the Space Shuttle Atlantis (STS-129) with an eventual destination of the International Space Station. Why? What kinds of things did they hope to learn by doing this?

Gravity affects so many things we do and how we do them, but we can only know whether some things are directly affected by gravity in the near-absence of it.

At the same time, the monarch caterpillars, which they called "astropillars," were blasting off, more than 400 classrooms, homeschoolers, and individuals who had received test kits from Monarch Watch, were conducting parallel experiments here on earth.

Behaviorally, monarchs are negatively geotactic, meaning they prefer to move upward against gravity. They also are positively phototactic, meaning they move towards light. During the Space Shuttle experiments, the three monarchs were observed as they progressed through their life stages to see if gravity was necessary for them to complete each stage.

The scientists had made predictions as to what they thought would happen, and for the most part they were correct. For example, they only expected the adult butterflies to live for about a week, and that's what happened, mainly attributed to their not being able to find or use the provided nectar feeder. All three caterpillars pupated successfully, and experienced eclosure, though one butterfly was not able to pump its wings fully of fluid like the other two.

What did they learn?

None of the developing chrysalides were able to attach the cremaster to the silk button and were floating freely within the container. All three

emerged from the chrysalis just fine, though they had some difficulty pumping the fluid into their wings. Two eventually filled their wings enough that they would have been able to fly; the third had wing deformities enough that it would have found flight difficult, if even possible. This could have been due to deformities in the chrysalis, conditions in space, or both.

The conclusion was that monarchs need gravity to properly execute pupation and eclosure and that gravity definitely plays a part in the proper expansion of the wings. More on the experiment can be found here: http://monarchwatch.org/space.

All in all, it was a wonderful way to get kids involved with nature in an inquisitive and different way, as well as understanding the role the space program plays in its quest to learn more about how things work on earth. 🦋

# Create a Monarch Waystation

In 2005, Monarch Watch started its Monarch Waystation program, encouraging citizens to create an oasis of milkweed and nectar plants that benefit monarchs, to help offset the decline in natural habitat throughout their spring and summer breeding range.

Locations for these waystations can be just about anywhere there's a patch of land available for planting: backyards, businesses, schools, universities, parks, churches, roadsides, nature centers and zoos.

Plant choices for a garden that will attract pollinators and monarchs in particular will of course include the family of milkweeds. But, while milkweed is their lone host plant and milkweed flowers are good nectar sources, it takes more than milkweed to sustain life in a garden made for monarchs.

Once they become adults, monarchs rely on nectar sources that are available during all the days of their lives. Special attention needs to be given to those flowers that bloom in the later part of the season, when the monarchs are migrating.

Registry: monarchwatch. org/waystations. They have waystation kits available, to make it even easier. And recently, they have expanded their program with the Monarch Waystation Network, which provides resources and support for educators, students and other non-profit organizations. See what's new at monarchwaystationnetwork. res.ku.edu/.

The Xerces Society also provides extensive lists of the best monarch nectar plants for a particular region, including bloom times and which varieties are likely to be commercially available: xerces.org/monarch-nectar-plants.

Nectar provides not only energy for the long trip to Mexico, but also for storing lipids in their abdomens, which gets them through the winter. The healthier monarchs are when they arrive at their overwintering locations, the greater their chances at surviving through spring, to give birth to the next year's population.

Of course, the plants that will grow in your garden may not grow in everyone's. Climate and soil types will influence your choices. Monarch Watch provides guidelines for creating a waystation, with planting suggestions, basic care instructions, and requirements for having the habitat certified and listed in the International Monarch Waystation

The simple garden plan shown here is only one example of possible designs and is specifically targeted to attract monarchs, but you'll find that it attracts quite a number of other pollinators too. It is created with USDA Hardiness Zones 5-6 in mind, as this growing zone is in the middle of North America. Many of the plants in this garden will also grow in other zones. If you don't know your growing zone, you can find it at planthardiness.ars. usda.gov/PHZMWeb. 🦋

# Monarch Garden Plan

Here is an example of a well-diversified pollinator and monarch garden. Your space may be smaller – or even larger – but the plants listed below are all tasty and nutritious for your monarch visitors.

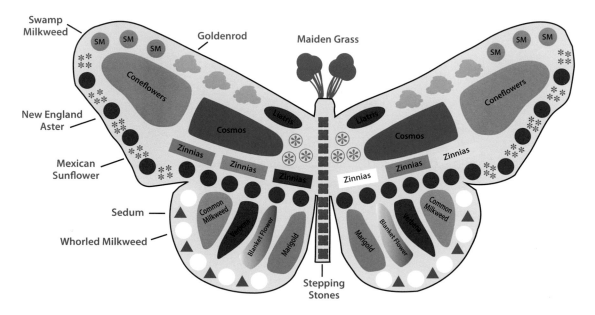

## Plant list key:

Blanket flower (*Gaillardia* spp.)
Blazing star (*Liatris ligulistylis*)
Brazilian verbena (*Verbena bonariensis*)
Common milkweed (*Asclepias syriaca*)
Maiden grass (*Miscanthus sinensis* 'Gracillimus')
Mexican sunflower (*Tithonia rotundifolia* 'Torch')
New England aster (*Symphyotrichum novae-angliae*)
Purple coneflower (*Echinacea purpurea*)
Showy goldenrod (*Solidago speciosa*)
Signet marigold (*Tagetes tenuifolia*)

Stonecrop sedum (*Hylotelephium spectabile* 'Autumn Fire')
Sulphur cosmos (*Cosmos sulphureus*)
Swamp milkweed (*Asclepias incarnata*)
Whorled milkweed (*Asclepias verticillata*)
Wild bergamot (*Monarda fistulosa*)
Zinnia   Multi-colored

*NOTE: You can, of course, substitute other species for the ones listed here. For example, another blazing star that will attract monarchs and provide nectar is **Liatris asperula**.*

# Make a Butterfly Watering Station

Much attention is paid to providing nectar sources for adult butterflies, but we know that they also need water and may be drawn to locations that supply it. Providing an accessible source of water close to their preferred nectar sources can be just one more way to attract monarchs to your garden, patio, porch or balcony.

You may have seen butterflies congregating at the edges of mud and water puddles to suck up water through their proboscises. They may be merely getting a drink, but some may also be doing so with another important purpose: In large groups, they are nearly always males, engaging in the act of "puddling." They're gathering salts and minerals from the water that will become incorporated into the spermatophore (the packet containing the sperm that they transfer to the female during mating). These nutrients will nourish the eggs, increasing the health and number of eggs that a female will lay.

If you don't have a way to help the monarchs by growing nectar plants or milkweed, this simple watering station can be a welcome refreshment for them on a hot summer's day.

## Supplies:

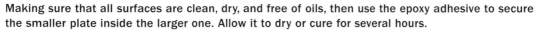

* **Two sizes of saucers or plates**
  (either garden pot saucers or kitchen plates
* **Epoxy or other weather-resistant adhesive**
* **Plant hanger**
* **Natural or decorative rocks**

Making sure that all surfaces are clean, dry, and free of oils, then use the epoxy adhesive to secure the smaller plate inside the larger one. Allow it to dry or cure for several hours.

Place pebbles or small rocks in the smaller plate. These allow the butterflies to have additional areas to sit while sipping the water. Add clean, fresh water.

A plant hanger allows you to hang the watering station up out of the way of pets or children, if necessary. You can also just set the station on the ground or on a table.

*Be sure to change the water daily to keep it clean for the butterflies and to avoid harboring mosquitoes.*

I chose a black salad plate and an orange pot saucer for my watering station, to mimic the monarch's colors, but you can use whatever you prefer. Thrift shops and garage sales are good places to find inexpensive materials or you may already have what you need right in your own home. 🦋

# Raise a Monarch in Your Home

Nothing brings home the miracle of metamorphosis like raising a butterfly egg in your home, where you can watch it up close in all its glory. It's pretty easy to be a monarch mama or papa, but there are some basic procedures to know and some helpful tips to go along with the process.

Before we get started on how to do things, let's talk a bit about the ethics of it. I've been questioned as to whether it's wise or even helpful to monarchs to bring them in the house to complete their life cycle. That's a valid question. I mean, Mother Nature knows best, right?

As I've mentioned elsewhere in this book, the survival rate for insects in general is low. For monarchs, it's downright dismal. Left in the wild, a monarch has about a 5% chance of making it to adulthood (and that's probably being generous). Raised indoors, that percentage is often reversed. My own experience is just that – 95% of the monarchs I have raised inside have been released as adults. And the 5% I lost were nearly all caterpillars that I'd brought in that had already been parasitized by the tachinid fly.

I'm not advocating that everyone bring in every monarch egg or caterpillar they can find, because not everyone will be dedicated enough or have enough time to keep containers clean and everyone

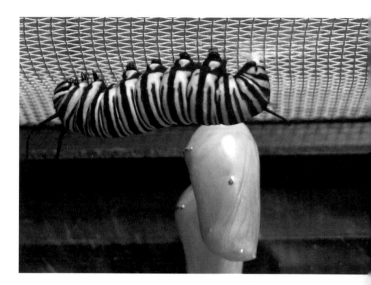

fed and happy with healthy milkweed. But raising one or two in your house is an eye-opening and wondrous work of nature to behold.

This is an especially good way to get children involved with caring for nature's creatures and developing a healthy respect for them. My own grandchildren were enthralled with the whole process at the young ages of two and three. Even at that age, it's fun for them to go looking for eggs and caterpillars in the garden or in fields, wherever milkweed is found.

## Where to look and what to look for

This is simple, really. Where there's milkweed, there could be monarchs. Look under the leaves especially, for eggs and first instar caterpillars. Larger caterpillars may be seen crawling just about anywhere on the plants. When you do find them, just break off the leaf they're on and take that, instead of trying to remove a caterpillar from it. It's easier to transfer them to milkweed you've provided at home just by laying the collected leaf on top of another one.

## Their home away from home

There are variations to this method of housing the caterpillars and chrysalides, but this is how I do it.

### *Supplies:*

(some you will use in the beginning, some later in the life cycle):

* Small shallow container such as a plastic storage container
* Paper towels
* Mesh container (sold for just this purpose) or glass or plastic container – a fish bowl, punch bowl, or small terrarium works well
* Plastic wrap or old pantyhose and rubber band
* Bud vase or small bottle, or florist's tubes
* Aluminum foil
* Toothpicks
* Twig

## The egg stage

Sometimes you'll find eggs, and sometimes you'll find caterpillars, in all stages of growth. It's best to bring monarchs inside at the earliest stage possible, to minimize vulnerability to predators.

When you get the leaf with your egg back to your house, rinse it off with lukewarm water, being careful not to rub the egg off. The water won't hurt the egg; after all, it rains outside.

If you're bringing in an egg (or very tiny caterpillar) you will want to first use something to house it that's small and shallow, such as a plastic storage container, to keep a close eye on things.

Cut a piece of paper towel to fit the bottom of the container, making sure even the edges can lie flat. Wet the paper towel just enough so that all the dry areas have absorbed some water. Don't soak it completely, as too much moisture once you've covered it will foster mold growth. This moist paper towel will help keep the milkweed leaf from drying out too much. Your new hatchling will want tender milkweed, not something dried out.

Press the wet paper towel to the bottom of the container, working out any air bubbles, especially along the edges. This is to assure that the newly-hatched caterpillar won't somehow get trapped under the edges when it wanders around.

Cover the container and secure it with a rubber band. Use a toothpick to poke air holes in the top. Don't make the holes too big, because even though the new caterpillars tend to stay on the milkweed and munch, once in a while you'll see them wandering about the container.

I use a bud vase filled with water with a piece of aluminum foil over the top. I poke a small hole in the center of the foil and then gently put the milkweed stem down through it. Remove any leaves that are low on the stem so they aren't in the water, because those will rot if you don't.

There are other ways to make sure your milkweed stays fresh for a day or two. You can use a wet paper towel and wrap that around the bottom of the stems and then cover the paper towel with aluminum foil. With this method, you can then just lay the milkweed down in the bottom of your container. Florist's tubes are even better, as they'll keep the stem in water, yet you can still lay the milkweed down if you want to.

## Caterpillar stage

When looking for monarch eggs outside, you'll come across a caterpillar now and then. In fact, this might be what you find most often, because they're so much easier to see. Again, just pinch off the whole leaf, or even snip the entire stem of the plant, if it's near the top. The plant will regrow and your caterpillar will eat the milkweed you bring it in on.

For caterpillars of any size, including those you've raised from the egg, you will want to use a larger container than you did for the leaves with eggs. I use a large punch bowl, but a fish bowl or terrarium works too. There are mesh containers made just for this purpose available as well.

When you get it inside, rinse the leaves all around the caterpillar. You may want to temporarily transfer the caterpillar to a dish while you prepare the milkweed for your housing container.

You'll find that caterpillars have ravenous appetites and with all that eating comes a whole lot of pooping. Their poop is called frass and you'll need to keep it cleaned out of the container on a daily basis.

*Tip:* Since a monarch caterpillar's diet consists of green leaves, that makes it a pretty efficient composting machine. When cleaning out the container, don't let that frass go to waste! Sprinkle it on top of the soil on your favorite houseplant. Don't worry – it doesn't smell bad and it will add a small amount of nutrients to the soil. It may not be enough to make much difference, but it won't hurt anything either.

As the caterpillar grows larger, it will outgrow its skin several times. When a caterpillar is preparing to molt (shed its skin), it will position itself somewhere and it won't move for sometimes as long as a day. You may worry that something is wrong with it, but don't disturb it! You'll soon see that it's fine, and if you watch at just the right time, you may get to witness it literally walking right out of its old skin.

The caterpillar will allow its new outer skin to firm up a bit and then it often will turn around and eat its old skin. It will molt a total of four times before it sheds its skin for the fifth and last time as it forms its chrysalis.

## Chrysalis stage

After about two weeks as a caterpillar, the monarch is ready for the final stage of becoming an adult butterfly. It will begin to wander about the container, seeking a place to pupate, usually at the top of the container,

on whatever you're using to cover it. If you've placed a stick in the container, they will often crawl to the upper end of that. When it has found a suitable location, it uses its spinneret to form a silk pad and a "button" from which it will hang.

Once the caterpillar has formed its silk pad and button, it will walk away from it until it can grab onto the button with its anal prolegs – the last pair at the back of its abdomen. Slowly it will let loose, starting at the head, and it will end up hanging in the "J" formation, upside down.

When you see the filaments at the head end become limp and twisted, pupation is ready to start any time. You may notice the head making some chewing movements and soon it will begin having contractions. Watch for the skin to split between the filaments, and enjoy the show!

As the skin gets to the top, watch for the black cremaster to pop out and embed itself in the silk button. The skin will fall off as the chrysalis wiggles about. Don't be alarmed if it doesn't fall off though. Sometimes it remains attached

at the very top. As long as it isn't constricting the chrysalis itself, it's okay to let it stay there. The butterfly will be emerging from the bottom.

## Eclosure

You've just witnessed the first miracle of metamorphosis! The monarch no longer looks like a caterpillar, in fact, you will probably be amazed at how quickly it changed from a caterpillar to a chrysalis. How long did that take exactly? Five minutes or so. But the best is yet to come!

In about 11-15 days, depending on the temperature, it will be time for the adult butterfly to emerge. Beginning approximately 24 hours before the big event, you'll see a continual darkening of the chrysalis until it's clear, revealing the colorful butterfly within.

When the time is right, you may notice a tiny bit of air space has formed between the butterfly and the cuticle of the chrysalis. Next, the outer part of the chrysalis will crack and you'll see the monarch pushing out. This happens very quickly, maybe over the span of a couple of minutes, so don't blink!

Once your monarch is out, it will begin pumping fluid into its wings as well as working to get the two parts of the proboscis zipped together. At this point, it's important that it be able to hang freely, as gravity assists with the proper formation of the wings. It doesn't happen often, but if it should fall and not be able to crawl back up to something, the wings will eventually dry in a crumpled form and it won't be able to fly. You can intervene and help it by coaxing it to grab onto your finger and then back onto the empty chrysalis or a surface where it can hang freely.

It will be several hours before you can release it, as those wings need time to dry and firm up. When you see it flexing its wings, it's probably pretty safe to let it climb onto your finger and take it outside.

If the weather happens to be stormy and very windy, you can wait a day or two before releasing it. If it's not extreme though, you can still release it in a protected location. Remember, they're made to withstand all sorts of weather.

They don't need to eat in the first 24 hours, but if you keep it longer, you can take a paper towel and soak it with fruit juice or use orange slices and place it in the rearing container. When it's hungry, you'll see it sipping with its proboscis. Release it when the weather is in a better mood.

## Bet you can't raise just one

The thing about raising one monarch is that it oftentimes leads to another and another and another. It can be compelling and addicting, this rush you get from seeing such a tiny egg hatch and the tiniest of caterpillars grow, form a chrysalis – only to bring forth a beautiful butterfly that bears no resemblance to the caterpillar it started out as.

However, if you do decide to raise monarchs in number inside your house or in any man-made habitat, there are other considerations to give to the process. There are a number of guides to help you, should you want to take this step, which I've listed in the reference section at the back of this book.

## Things to remember:

✳ Wash your hands and rinse thoroughly. Don't handle milkweed or the monarchs if you've used any kind of lotion, as it could be toxic to the monarchs. In fact, be hypervigilant when it comes to any kind of chemical used in your home near where you're raising monarchs, even air freshener.

✳ The only safe thing to clean the containers with is a dilute chlorine bleach solution (1 part regular chlorine bleach to 19 parts water) or just plain water. Other cleaners may be harmful to the monarchs.

✳ Try not to handle your caterpillars any more than you have to, especially the really tiny ones. When transferring them to fresh milkweed, I trim the older leaf around the caterpillar carefully and then lay it on the new leaf. Once the caterpillar has moved onto the new one, I throw out the old one.

✳ You can store cut milkweed in the refrigerator so that you have some on hand for several days. Just wash it off, pat dry, then wrap in damp paper towels. Put them in a plastic bag and keep in the crisper drawer of your refrigerator.

✳ When handling older caterpillars, I often use a toothpick or a cotton swab to gently lift them off whatever they're on. You'll find that they're very tenacious when hanging onto leaves, the side of the container or twigs, and you don't want to injure those tiny body parts. 🦋

# How to Tag a Migrating Monarch

The tagging program administered by Monarch Watch through the University of Kansas is one of the most well-known citizen-science programs. The researchers depend on a large number of ordinary citizens of all ages to help with the tagging so that they can use the data collected to help answer several important questions about monarch migration:

* Where do the monarchs begin their journey?
* When do they begin?
* How long does it take them to complete the trip south?
* How fast can they travel?
* What is their mortality during migration?
* Which route do they take while traveling from here to there?

Monarchs that are recovered in Mexico are ones that have survived the journey, but for some reason didn't live once they got there. Local residents find them and are paid a small amount of money for turning in found tags from expired monarchs. The identification numbers are then recorded with Monarch Watch.

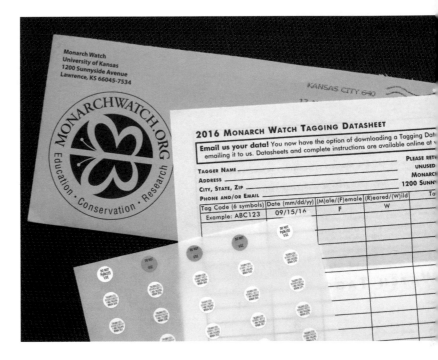

Any monarchs that are found elsewhere on the migration route are also reported, whether it be ones that are no longer living or merely observed while on their way to Mexico.

The tags are about as big around as the end of a pencil eraser and are self-stick. They are relatively weatherproof and were developed over many, many years to be long lasting, while not harming the monarch or interfering with its flight.

## To tag a monarch:

First, prepare the tag. I use the end of a toothpick to pull the tag off the sheet, because you don't want to get skin oils on the adhesive. Tweezers work well, too. Lay the toothpick aside.

Grasp the monarch while it sits at rest, with all four wings held over its body. Be sure to hold all four wings between your index finger and your thumb, and lift it gently from whatever it's resting on. It will want to hang on to whatever that is, and lifting it too quickly could damage its tarsal claws on the end of its legs.

Take the toothpick with the tag on it and lay it on the discal cell of one of the hind (lower) wings. You'll recognize this cell as the one that looks a little like a mitten. Place the tag in the middle of that cell and then use your thumb to hold it in place while rolling the end of the toothpick away. Continue to hold the tag in place between your thumb and index finger for about five seconds.

Should you somehow miss getting it in just the right spot, don't try to take it off and move it. You'll only risk damaging the wing and most certainly remove some of the scales. Just leave it where it is and try to do better with the next one.

That's all there is to it! Don't forget to record the date, location, sex and tag ID number on your data sheet. You can now release your monarch and wish it well on its journey. It may stick around for a little while, perhaps even for a day or so, but it will soon take flight and be on its way.

While tagging monarchs can be personally fun to do, with the hopes that "our" monarchs might be found in Mexico, please remember that this is scientific work that we are participating in. Researchers are counting heavily on taggers to follow tagging and data reporting instructions. It's not difficult at all, and the biggest reward comes from the knowledge the researchers gain from the tagging program – knowledge that will aid all of us with our endeavor to help the monarch population thrive.

For more information about the tagging program and how you can participate, see the tagging program page on Monarch Watch's website: monarchwatch.org/tagmig/tag.htm 🦋

The tag on the monarch butterfly's wing reads:

TAG@KU.EDU
MONARCH WATCH
1-888-TAGGING
UMY 375

# *Make a Monarch Bracelet*

We've attended the Monarch Festival at Eagle Marsh Preserve in Ft. Wayne, Indiana, on numerous occasions. It's a wonderful family

event held every September, where you can learn all about the life cycle of the monarch, plant milkweed, take a free plant home for your own garden, and even tag migrating monarchs and send them on their way.

The last time we went, we took our grandson Anthony, and at one of the learning stations he made a monarch life-cycle bracelet. What a wonderful way to teach all four stages in the life of the monarch butterfly! This bracelet is inspired by the one Anthony made that day. The concept is simple and making the bracelet is too.

## Supplies:

❀ Pony beads* or 6 mm craft beads in white, black, yellow, green, metallic gold, orange and clear

❀ .5mm (or larger, depending on size of hole in beads) stretchy cord in black or transparent

## Instructions:

Cut a length of the stretchy cord 4" longer than the circumference of your wrist

String beads onto the cord in the following order:

{
Clear
White – represents the egg,
   the first stage in the life cycle
Clear
}

{
Yellow
Black – represents the caterpillar,
   the second stage in the life cycle
White
}

{
Clear
Green – represents the chrysalis,
   the third stage in the life cycle
Metallic gold – represents the gold spots
   on the chrysalis
Clear
}

{
Orange
White – represents the adult butterfly
Black
}

Depending on the size of the bracelet and the size of the beads, you may be able to repeat the bead sequence to make a solid beaded bracelet. Another option is to use clear beads to finish it out.

Tie the two ends of the stretchy cord around the wrist to fit, using three knots to make it secure. Trim the ends.

*Optional:* Place a dot of glue on the knotted ends for extra security.

*If you use pony beads, you can use a black pipe cleaner on which to string the beads instead of the stretchy cord, as they have a larger diameter hole for stringing. If you use a pipe cleaner, be sure to make the bracelet large enough to slip on and off the wrist, and use pliers to bend the sharp wire ends over. 🐝

# Make a Monarch Butterfly Ring

Here's a quick and fun little craft that kids will love. I've made these for my own grandkids and even the youngest ones will wear them for hours.

## Supplies:

- **Colored card stock or construction paper**
- **Pipe cleaners**
- **Scissors**
- **Needle-nose pliers (optional)**

Trace one of each size of the butterfly patterns onto the card stock or construction paper and cut them out. (I use card stock because it's sturdier and will last longer.)

Place the smaller one on top of the larger one, centering it.

Carefully use the tip of the scissors to make two holes in the center of the two butterflies, about a quarter-inch apart.

Cut a length of pipe cleaner 3-4" long and thread it through the holes in the butterflies, putting each end in the holes from the top side. Pull all the way through so that on the back side, the lengths of pipe cleaner are the same on each side.

Use the needle-nose pliers to bend the cut ends of the pipe cleaner tightly back on themselves so as to lessen the sharpness of the finished ends. Wrap the ends of the pipe cleaner around each other, forming a ring.

Bend the upper butterfly wings up slightly to give the butterfly a 3-D effect.

# Stir Up a Milkweed Cocktail

## Drink your milkweed!

Think milkweed is just good for bees and butterflies? Think again. According to Ellen Zachos, author of *The Wildcrafted Cocktail*, milkweed provides many edible opportunities for us, too.

"I consider milkweed to be a wild edible superstar because it has so many delicious parts," Ellen says. "The young shoots, stripped of their leaves, are edible in spring, and I think they taste better than green beans. The unopened flower buds are equally tasty and should be harvested before they show any color. The flowers make a uniquely-flavored syrup, and the underripe pods are at their best in mid- to late summer."

*\*Ellen notes, "All parts of milkweed, except the ripe flowers, should be blanched before cooking them in any recipe. That stops the flow of their white sap. And as with any new food (whether it's foraged or from Whole Foods), start small. An allergic or toxic reaction is easier to manage if you only eat a small quantity."*

*Be aware that some people have been sickened by eating raw or unblanched milkweed pods and leaves.*

Ellen shares this recipe for a milkweed cocktail (for the grownups!):

### A Butterfly's Kiss

**2 ½ ounces vodka**
**1½ ounces milkweed simple syrup**
**½ ounce sparkling water or club soda**
**A squeeze of lemon**

Combine the vodka and milkweed simple syrup in a shaker full of ice and shake for 30 seconds. Strain into a glass and top with sparkling water or club soda. Finish with a squeeze of lemon.

Non-alcoholic version: **Combine equal parts milkweed simple syrup and sparkling water and add a squeeze of lemon. Adjust proportions to suit your taste.**

**To make milkweed simple syrup:**

Combine ½ cup of fresh, open milkweed flowers with ½ cup of sugar and mix well. Seal the flower sugar in a tightly closed container. After 24 hours, transfer the sugar and flowers to a saucepan and add ½ cup of water. Heat the mixture until the sugar completely dissolves (it doesn't have to boil) and whisk to avoid scorching. Remove from the heat and let sit another 24 hours. Strain the flowers out and discard them. The syrup will keep for several weeks in the refrigerator.

**Cheers!**

# Projects for Those Who Teach

Whether you're a parent, a 4-H advisor, or a teacher in a classroom, opportunities to help others learn present themselves pretty often. Here are a few project suggestions.

## Symbolic Migration – Uniting Children Across North America

Since 1995, Journey North has been helping teachers help their students learn about the monarch's migration through their Symbolic Migration Program. In the fall, classroom students throughout North America make decorative monarch butterflies and send them to other children who live near the monarch sanctuaries in Mexico – coinciding with the time of the actual monarch migration.

Those children, in turn, take care of the symbolic monarchs and return them with personal notes to their northern classrooms in the spring, when the real monarchs are beginning their journey north. What a wonderful way to join the three countries where the monarch resides – Canada, United States and Mexico – while everyone learns more about the monarchs!

For more information, see the Journey North website: learner.org/jnorth/sm

## Teachers Pay Teachers – teacherspayteachers.com/Browse/Search:monarch%20butterfly

This is an incredible resource for those who want to teach…well… just about anything! Quite a number of these teaching aids from teacher members are free, and many more require a small fee. When I did a search for "monarch butterfly," I got 440 results. If you can't find what you want to help your child learn about butterflies in a fun way here, I doubt it exists.

### Grants for School Gardens

If you've ever visited a school garden, you know how much the kids love working in it. They're so proud of what they're doing, not just because of the wow factor of growing things they can actually eat, but because for some, this is their first exposure to gardening. Butterflies have to eat too, and where better for kids to nurture the monarch and other pollinators than in a garden they created and cared for?

There are several opportunities to apply for grants that will help establish or maintain a school garden or nature area. Most of these, if not all, sponsor grants each year:

* **Wild Ones** – wildones.org/seeds-for-education/sfe
* **Whole Kids Foundation** – wholekidsfoundation.org/schools/programs/school-garden-grant-program
* **Lowe's Toolbox for Education** – toolboxforeducation.com
* **Annie's Grants for Gardens** – annies.com/giving-back/school-gardens/grants-for-gardens
* **Project Learning Tree Greenworks Grants** – plt.org/resources/greenworks-grants
* **Scotts Miracle-Gro Grassroots Grant** – scottsmiraclegro.com/responsibility/gro1000
* **Monarch Lab Schoolyard Garden Grants** – monarchlab.org/education-and-gardening/gardening-for-monarchs/garden-grants
* **Kids Gardening** – kidsgardening.org/garden-grants

### 4-H Projects

As a young person who spent many years in 4-H, I remember to this day some of the projects I took on. I most especially remember my first flower garden. It was likely where I saw my first monarch butterfly up close. There are still gardening projects in the 4-H curriculum today for learning how to create a pollinator garden, but there are also projects about butterflies and other insects, which can be tailored to the monarch: Project Butterfly Wings and Teaming With Insects I, II, and III.

FIRST OFFICER
LEROY
HOMER
AUGUST 27, 1965
SEPTEMBER 11, 2001

IN HONOR OF
THE CREW
UNITED AIRLINES
FLIGHT 93
SEPTEMBER 11, 2001

FOREVER IN OUR HEARTS

# Epilogue: The Rest of the Story

✣

Remember that tagged monarch butterfly my mother found in 2006 in Shanksville, Pennsylvania? The story didn't end there, but it would be ten years before I learned more about it.

When we returned home from that trip, I visited the Monarch Watch website and reported the recovery of the tagged monarch. Since it was the beginning of the tagging season, Monarch Watch had not yet received the tagging data from the person to whom the tags were sent – and they would not assemble data for that season until the following spring.

I forgot about checking on it and life kept me busy. Until October 2016. That's when I decided to finally follow up with it. All Monarch Watch could tell me was that the tag had been distributed to someone in Clarksburg, Pennsylvania.

I put my detective hat on and first looked to see how large a city Clarksburg was. With a population of approximately 1,500, this increased my chance of finding the person who had applied that tag to that particular butterfly.

Monarch Watch's Waystation program was begun in 2005, and I figured anyone who was into monarch tagging probably had their property registered as a waystation. So, I consulted their registry, which is available for viewing online, and in the more than 15,000 registered waystations, only one was listed for Clarksburg, registered in August of 2006. I decided to try to contact the owner.

Starting with the assumption that the name Cunkelman in "Cunkelman's Safe Haven" referred to the owner's last name, I coupled it with "Clarksburg," and did a Google search. One of the items shown was a 2013 Seedlings newsletter from District VI of the Garden Club Federation of Pennsylvania. Not only was a Marcy Cunkelman the newsletter's editor, there was also a notice in

it that she would be hosting an open house in her garden, as well as a link to a video that a local TV station filmed there, showing Marcy demonstrating how to tag a monarch.

Though Marcy's email was provided in the newsletter, I looked to see if by chance she was on Facebook. Sure enough she was, so I private messaged her, asking if the monarch my mother found could possibly have been tagged by her. I could not have imagined the answer that I received two days later.

Yes, the monarch was tagged with one of her tags, but this was a very special tagging. Her garden club maintained the Children's Peace Garden by the Memorial Chapel in Shanksville. On the fifth anniversary of the United Flight 93 crash, a ceremony was held there to dedicate the monument and many of the crash victims' families were in attendance.

Marcy had brought seven tagged monarchs to be released from the garden and she asked those family members if they would like to release the monarchs. They did, and those who released them included the spouses of the captain and first officer of the crew of Flight 93.

What a special story that little monarch had to tell.

🦋

In the years since my mother picked up Marcy's tagged monarch at the Flight 93 memorial, I have been on a journey of discovery. My relationship with the monarch was more than just your average level of interest. I went down so many rabbit holes as I learned first one thing and then another. This was no simple insect. But then, none of them really are.

There's a word for when you learn something and then all of sudden you see it everywhere, when you never really did before. It's called Baader-Meinhof phenomenon and that's just a fancy name for one of a million unique ways the brain works. When you learn something new, it stays in the forefront of your mind for a while and your brain pays special attention to it. Even though it's been there all along, your brain may have dismissed it because it didn't have relevance for you.

Monarchs started appearing everywhere for me. I would have dismissed it as this quirky syndrome, if that's all it was. But monarchs really WERE everywhere. Everywhere except my gardens and everyone else's.

On the internet, in the newspapers, on television, on the radio – concern over the decline in the monarch population was starting to show up here and there. The situation was not good, but there was a bright spot at the end of it all. Just as we humans were partially to blame for fewer monarchs, we could also be part of the solution.

Scientists, biologists, environmentalists, and a whole slew of people who were concerned and studying the situation had sounded the alarm and they needed our help. There aren't many such widespread issues whose direction can be changed by ordinary people like you and me, or in which

people truly believe that anything they do will have any measurable effect.

But reversing the decline in the number of monarchs is one where we really can make a difference. I hope that I've shown you at least some ways you can participate. I hope I've motivated you to want to – and to start on your own journey of discovery. 🦋

*No one is an environmentalist by birth. It is only your path, your life, your travels that awaken you.*

~Yann Arthus-Bertrand, photographer and creator of the book *Earth from Above* and the film Home.

# Appendix

# Glossary

**ABDOMEN:** the largest part of the monarch's main body, located behind the thorax.

**ANDROCONIAL SCALES:** the two black spots on the hind wings of the male monarch butterfly. They are believed to be involved in some way with mating.

**ANTENNA (plural – antennae):** the two conspicuous sensory appendages on the monarch's head used to navigate, touch and smell. The ends are clubbed, a characteristic of most butterflies. The antennae also emit a pheromone to aid in attracting a mate.

**APOSEMATISM:** the mechanism of bright colors and patterns on an organism signaling they are poisonous or distasteful.

**ARMY:** the term used for a group of caterpillars.

***ASCLEPIAS:*** the genus of plants known as milkweed. There are over 140 known species and it is the only genus used by monarch butterflies for feeding their young.

**BASKING:** being cold-blooded, butterflies bask in the sun to help raise their body temperature for flying.

**BROOD:** the term used to denote a single generation of butterflies.

**BRUSHFOOT:** the small forelegs closest to the head in a particular group of butterflies. Brushfeet are used to scratch the surface of potential food sources as a means of identification. Brushfoot butterflies are often called four-footed butterflies because the brushfeet are carried close to the body and aren't easily seen.

**BUTTON:** the thickened spot of silk in the middle of the silk pad that the monarch creates in order to attach itself when hanging in the J position, just prior to forming a chrysalis. During chrysalis formation, the cremaster will become embedded in the silk button.

**CAT:** among butterfly enthusiasts, a common abbreviation for caterpillar.

**CARDENOLIDES (also called cardiac glycosides):** A toxin contained in the latex (sap) and leaves of milkweeds which affects the heart. Monarchs have the ability to sequester this toxin within their bodies so that it doesn't affect them. It affords them some protection from predators who would be poisoned by it. Some milkweeds are more toxic than others.

**CELL:** a section of a monarch's wing that is bordered by veins.

**CHEMORECEPTORS:** nerve cells on a monarch's body that detect chemicals in their environment, such as nectar and pheromones.

**CHITIN:** the exoskeleton of insects and other arthropods are composed of this tough substance.

**CHORION:** the outer shell of the egg which protects the developing larva within.

**CHRYSALIS:** the semi-hard outer casing that forms when a butterfly caterpillar molts for the final time. Inside the chrysalis is the developing pupa. In the monarch, the chrysalis is a light emerald green, dotted with gold and black spots.

**CLASPERS:** two appendages at the far end of a male monarch which are used to grasp the female during mating.

**CLUB:** the thickened end of an antennae.

**COCOON:** the silk covering created by a moth caterpillar when it pupates.

**COMA:** another word for the white floss contained within a milkweed seed pod.

**CREMASTER:** a black stem-like structure on the posterior end of the pupa containing tiny hooks, which attach to the silk button, enabling the chrysalis to hang in suspension.

**CROCHETS:** tiny hooks on the end of the abdominal prolegs of a caterpillar.

**DIAPAUSE:** a period of reduced or halted development during any life stage of an organism. The migrational generation of monarchs eclose in a state of reproductive diapause, and will not sexually develop until much later, in spring, as they begin the migration northward.

**DISCAL CELL:** the cell located in the middle of a wing that is mostly free of veins. On the monarch, the discal cell resembles a mitten.

**DIURNAL:** active during the day. Nearly all butterflies are diurnal.

**DORSAL:** a term denoting the top side.

**ECDYSIS:** the process of molting.

**ECLOSE:** to emerge from the chrysalis as an adult butterfly.

**EXOSKELETON:** an external, protective covering. When a monarch caterpillar molts, it sheds its exoskeleton.

**EXUVIA:** the outer exoskeleton that is left over after molting.

**EYE SPOTS:** round patterns on a caterpillar or butterfly that resemble eyes that serve to deceive predators and aid in survival.

**FECUND:** the ability to produce offspring in abundant numbers. A female monarch's fecundity is measured by the number of eggs she produces.

**FILAMENTS:** antenna-like appendages on caterpillars, sometimes called tentacles. Monarch caterpillars have a set of two filaments on each end.

**FOREWINGS:** the two upper wings of a butterfly or moth.

**FRASS:** insect excrement that is the byproduct of eating. Caterpillar poop.

**GRAVID:** a female that has successfully mated with a male and is pregnant or carrying eggs.

**GENUS:** Every organism is classified and named according to a binomial nomenclature method created by the Swedish botanist Carl Linnaeus, in 1735. In this two-name system, the first name is the genus and the second name is the species. Each genus contains one or more species. Monarchs of North America are *Danaus plexippus*, with *Danaus* being the genus, and plexippus being the species. The genus is capitalized, the species is not, and both are always italicized. The plural of genus is genera.

**GONADS:** the male sex organs.

**HEMOLYMPH:** an insect's "blood."

**HINDWINGS:** the two lower wings of a butterfly.

**HOLDFAST TUBERCLES:** the lower black bumps at the top of a chrysalis that help hold it onto its silk pad, while the cremaster works its hooks into the silk button.

**IMAGINAL DISCS:** groups of cells within a caterpillar that will become the adult butterfly body parts.

**IMAGO:** the name for the fully-developed adult form of an insect.

**INSECTIVORE:** an organism whose diet includes insects.

**INSTAR:** the term given to the stages of growth through which a caterpillar goes before pupating. The monarch caterpillar experiences five instars, shedding its exoskeleton (molting) between each one.

**INVERTEBRATES:** the group of organisms that has no backbone. Butterflies are invertebrates.

**KALEIDOSCOPE:** the term used for a group of butterflies. Also used: rabble, swarm.

**LARVA (plural – larvae):** the caterpillar stage in the life cycle of a butterfly or moth.

**LABIAL PALPS:** the two mustache-like structures on each side of the proboscis. Shortly after eclosing, the monarch uses the palps to help press the two parts of the proboscis together. Throughout the rest of its life, the labial palps assist the monarch in a sensory way, in regard to tasting.

**LEGS:** Butterflies have six legs. These three pairs of legs are attached to the thorax, one pair in each segment. The first pair are the brushfeet, which you don't usually see, because they keep them tucked close to their body most of the time.

**LEPIDOPTERA:** the order of insects to which butterflies and moths belong. Literally means "scaly wing."

**LIFE CYCLE:** the stages of growth, from birth to death. In the monarch and other butterflies, the life cycle consists of egg, larva, pupa and adult.

**MANDIBLES:** the jaws of the caterpillar which bite off plant material for consumption. Adult butterflies don't have mandibles; they receive their (liquid) nourishment through their proboscis.

**MECONIUM:** the fluid that is expelled in the final stages of metamorphosis. It can be observed just below the newly-eclosed butterfly as a drop of brown liquid.

**METAMORPHOSIS:** the process of changing from a caterpillar to a butterfly.

**MIGRATION:** the seasonal movement of a particular species to a habitat that is more favorable, generally due to cold weather which they would not be able to survive.

**MIMICRY:** the close resemblance of one organism to another that gives them a particular advantage, for example, to obtain a mate or avoid predators.

**MOLTING:** the process of shedding the outer skin (exoskeleton), which has been outgrown during the larval stage of growth.

**NECTAR:** the sweet liquid contained in many flowers, from which several organisms derive their nutrition.

**NOCTURNAL:** active at night. Most moths are nocturnal.

**OCELLI:** a caterpillar's eyes.

**OE or *Ophryocystis elektroscirrha*:** OE is a naturally-occurring protozoan parasite found in nature that is particularly detrimental to the monarch butterfly.

**OMMATIDIA:** the light receptors on a butterfly's compound eyes. Each compound eye contains approximately 20,000 ommatidia.

**OMNIVORE:** an organism whose diet consists of both plants and animals.

**OVIPAROUS:** an organism that lays eggs that develop outside the mother's body.

**OVIPOSITOR:** a tubular organ at the end of the female's abdomen through which she deposits her eggs. The act of laying eggs is called ovipositing.

**OVUM:** egg.

**PARASITOID:** a type of predator, one that uses another organism as a host and whose larvae kill the host.

**PHEROMONE:** a chemical secreted by an organism to affect the behavior of another. Pheromones play an important role in animal and insect mating.

**POLLEN:** tiny grains containing the male reproductive cells of flowers.

**POLLINATOR:** an animal or insect that transfers pollen from flower to flower. Wind is also a pollinator.

**PREDATORS:** insects or animals that stalk, kill and feed on their prey.

**PROBOSCIS:** the coiled tube from which a butterfly or moth obtains liquid nourishment or nectar.

**PROLEG:** fleshy leg-like structures on the abdomen of the larval form of some insects.

**PROTHORAX:** the anterior segment of the thorax which bears the first pair of insect legs. In the monarch, this is where the brushfeet are attached.

**PUDDLING:** the act of male butterflies gathering at mud puddles or on other moist surfaces for the purpose of taking in salts and minerals which are then incorporated into the spermatophore, the packet that the male transfers to the female during mating.

**PUPA:** the third stage in the life cycle of a butterfly in which the developing butterfly is encased by a chrysalis.

**RABBLE:** A group of butterflies, also known as a kaleidoscope or swarm.

**SCALES:** modified hairs that cover a butterfly's wings, aiding in flight and giving the butterfly its colorful patterns.

**SEGMENTS:** the ring-like sections of a caterpillar's abdomen.

**SETAE:** tiny hairs on a monarch's body. The setae are attached to nerve cells, which relay tactile information to the monarch's brain, including touch and smell.

**SPERMATOPHORE:** packet of nutrients and salts along with sperm that is transferred to the female during mating. The nutrients and salts are used to provide nourishment to the eggs, thereby improving their survival.

**SPINNERET:** the silk-producing gland found just below a caterpillar's mouth.

**SPIRACLE:** the small oval openings on the sides of caterpillars and on the chrysalis through which the monarch takes in oxygen and expels carbon dioxide.

**TARSAL CLAWS:** the tiny hooks on the ends of a butterfly's feet – used to scratch the surface of leaves to taste, making sure they have the right plant.

**TARSUS:** a butterfly foot.

**THORAX:** the middle section of an insect's body, between the head and the abdomen.

**TUBERCLE:** any small, rounded projection on the surface of an animal or plant.

**ULTRAVIOLET LIGHT:** light rays invisible to human beings but visible to butterflies, that allow butterflies to see patterns on flowers, helping them locate food.

**VENTRAL:** a term denoting the underneath side.

**VEINS:** the slender tubes in the wings of butterflies/moths that provide nourishment by carrying the hemolymph (blood) to them. They also help provide support for the wings.

**WINGSPAN:** the distance measured across the wings.

# Native Milkweed Species, Their Range & Status

| | Botanical name | Common name | Native range |
|---|---|---|---|
| | *Asclepias albicans* | Whitestem milkweed | CA, AZ |
| * | *Asclepias amplexicaulis* | Clasping milkweed | AL, AR, CT, DC, DE, GA, IA, IL, IN, KS, KY, MA, MD, MI, MN, MO, MS, NC, NE, NH (Threatened), NJ, NY, OH, OK, PA, RI (Special Concern), SC, TN, VA, VT (Threatened), WI, WV |
| | *Asclepias angustifolia* | Arizona milkweed | AZ |
| * | *Asclepias arenaria* | Sand milkweed | CO, KS, NE, NM, OK, SD, TX, WY |
| * | *Asclepias asperula* | Antelope horns milkweed | AZ, CA, CO, ID, KS, NE, NM, NV, OK, TX , UT |
| | *Asclepias brachystephana* | Bracht milkweed | AZ, NM, TX |
| ** | *Asclepias californica* | California milkweed | Central and southern California |
| | *Asclepias cinerea* | Carolina milkweed | AL, FL, GA, MS, SC |
| | *Asclepias connivens* | Largeflower milkweed | AL, FL, GA, MS, SC |
| | *Asclepias cordifolia* | Heartleaf milkweed | CA, NV, OR |
| ** | *Asclepias cryptoceras* | Pallid milkweed | AZ, CA, CO, ID, OR, NV, WA, WY, UT |
| | *Asclepias curtissii* | Curtiss's milkweed | FL (Endangered) |
| | *Asclepias cutleri* | Cutler's milkweed | AZ, UT |
| | *Asclepias emoryi* | Emory's milkweed | NM, TX |
| * | *Asclepias engelmanniana* | Engelmann's milkweed | AZ, CO, IA (Endangered), KS, NE, NM, OK, TX, UT, WY |
| ** | *Asclepias eriocarpa* | Woolly pod milkweed | CA, NV, Baja California (Mexico) |
| ** | *Asclepias erosa* | Desert milkweed | AZ , CA , NV , UT |
| | *Asclepias exaltata* | Poke milkweed | AL, CT, DE, GA, IA, IL, IN, KY, MA, MD, ME, MI, MN, MS, NC, NH, NJ, NY, OH, PA, RI (Special Concern), SC, TN, VA, VT, WI, WV and ON, QC (Canada) |
| * | *Asclepias fascicularis* | Narrowleaf milkweed | CA , ID , NV , OR , UT , WA and Baja California (Mexico) |
| | *Asclepias feayi* | Florida milkweed | FL |
| ** | *Asclepias glaucescens* | Nodding milkweed | AZ, NM, TX |
| | *Asclepias hallii* | Hall's milkweed | AZ, CO, NM, NV, UT, WY |
| * | *Asclepias hirtella* | Green milkweed | AL, AR, GA, IA, IL, IN, KS, KY, LA, MI (Threatened), MN (Threatened), MO, OH, OK, TN (Special Concern),WI, WV, and ON (Canada) |
| | *Asclepias humistrata* | Pinewoods milkweed | AL, FL, GA, LA, MS, NC, SC |
| | *Asclepias hypoleuca* | Mahogany milkweed | AZ, NM |

| | | | |
|---|---|---|---|
| * | *Asclepias incarnata* | Swamp milkweed | AL, AR, CO, CT, DC, DE, FL, GA, IA, ID, IL, IN, KS, KY, LA, MA, MD, ME, MI, MN, MO, MT, NC, ND, NE, NH , NJ , NM, NV, NY, OH, OK, PA, RI, SC, SD, TN , TX , UT , VA , VT, WI, WV, WY and MB, NB, NS, ON, PE, QC (Canada) |
| | *Asclepias involucrata* | Dwarf milkweed | AZ, CO, KS, NM, OK, TX,  UT |
| | *Asclepias labriformis* | Utah milkweed | UT |
| | Asclepias lanceolata | Fewflower milkweed | AL, DC, FL, GA, LA, MD, MS, NC, NJ, SC, TN, TX, VA |
| | *Asclepias lanuginosa* | Sidecluster milkweed | IA (Threatened), IL (Endangered), KS, NE, ND, SD, WI (Threatened) and MB (Canada) |
| * | *Asclepias latifolia* | Broadleaf milkweed | AZ, CA, CO, KS, NE, NM, OK, SD, TX |
| | *Asclepias lemmonii* | Lemmon's milkweed | AZ |
| ** | *Asclepias linaria* | Pineneedle milkweed | AZ, CA, NM |
| | *Asclepias linearis* | Slim milkweed | DC, MD, TX |
| | *Asclepias longifolia* | Longleaf milkweed | AL, AR, DC, DE, FL, GA, LA, MD, MS, NC, SC, TX, VA, WV |
| | *Asclepias macrotis* | Longhood milkweed | AZ, CO, NM, OK, TX |
| | *Asclepias meadii* | Mead's milkweed | IA (Endangered), IL (Endangered), IN (Reintroduced), KS, MO (Endangered), WI - Federally Threatened |
| | *Asclepias michaux* | Michaux's milkweed | AL, FL, GA, LA, MS, SC |
| | *Asclepias nummularia* | Tufted milkweed | AZ, NM, TX |
| | *Asclepias nyctaginifolia* | Mohave milkweed | AZ, CA, NV, NM |
| | *Asclepias obovata* | Pineland milkweed | AL, AR, FL, GA, LA, MS, OK, SC, TX |
| ** | *Asclepias oenotheroides* | Zizotes milkweed | AZ, CO, LA, NM, OK, TX |
| * | *Asclepias ovalifolia* | Dwarf milkweed | IA, IL (Endangered), MI (Endangered), MN, ND, SD, WI (Threatened), WY, MT and BC, AL, SK, MB, ON (Canada) |
| | *Asclepias pedicellata* | Savannah milkweed | FL, GA, NC, SC |
| | *Asclepias perennis* | Aquatic milkweed | AL, AR, FL, GA, IL, IN, KY, LA, MO, MS, SC, TN, TX |
| | *Asclepias prostrata* | Prostrate milkweed | TX |
| * | *Asclepias pumila* | Plains milkweed | CO, IA, KS, MT, NE, ND, NM, OK, SD, TX, WY |
| * | *Asclepias purpurascens* | Purple milkweed | AR, CT (Special Concern), DC, DE, GA, IA, IL, IN, KS, KY, LA, MA (Endangered), MD, MI, MN, MO, MS, NC, NE, NH, NJ, N , OH, OK, PA, RI, SD, TN (Special Concern), TX, VA, WI (Endangered), WV |
| * | *Asclepias quadrifolia* | Four-leaved milkweed | AL, AR, CT, DC, DE, GA, IA, IL, IN, KS, KY, MA, MD, MI, MN, MO, MS, NC, NH (Threatened), NJ, OH, OK, PA, RI (Threatened), SC, TN, VA, VT, WI, WV, and ON (Canada) |
| | *Asclepias quinquedentata* | Slimpod milkweed | AZ, NM, TX |

| | | | |
|---|---|---|---|
| | *Asclepias rubra* | Red milkweed | AL, AR, DC, DE, FL, GL, GA, LA, MD (Endangered), MS, NC, NJ, NY, PA (Extirpated), SC, TX, VA, WV |
| | *Asclepias rusbyi* | Rusby's milkweed | AZ, CO, NM, NV, UT |
| | *Asclepias scaposa* | Bear mountain milkweed | TX, NM |
| | *Asclepias solanoana* | Serpentine milkweed | CA |
| * | *Asclepias speciosa* | Showy milkweed | AZ, CA, CO, IA (Threatened), ID, IL, KS, MI, MN, MT, ND, NE, NM, NV, OK, OR, SD, TX, UT, WA, WI, WY and AB, BC, MB, SK (Canada) |
| | *Asclepias sperryi* | Sperry's milkweed | TX |
| * | *Asclepias stenophylla* | Slimleaf milkweed | AR, CO, IA (Endangered), IL (Endangered), KS, LA, NE, MN (Endangered), MO, MT, OK, SD, TX, WY |
| * * | *Asclepias subulata* | Rush milkweed | AZ, CA, NV |
| * * | *Asclepias subverticillata* | Horsetail milkweed | AZ, CO, ID, KS, MT, NE, NM, MO, OK, TX, UT |
| * | *Asclepias sullivantii* | Sullivant's milkweed | AR, IA, IL, IN, KS, MI (Threatened), MN (Threatened), MO, ND, NE, OH, OK, SD, WI (Threatened), and ON (Canada) |
| * | *Asclepias syriaca* | Common milkweed | AL, AR, CT, DC, DE, GA, IA, IL, IN, KS, KY, LA, MA, MD, ME, MI, MN, MO, MS, MT, NC, ND, NE, NH, NJ, NY, OH, OK, OR, PA, RI, SC, SD, TN, TX, VA, VT, WI, WV and MB, NB, NS, ON, PE, QC, SK (Canada) |
| | *Asclepias texana* | Texas milkweed | TX |
| | *Asclepias tomentosa* | Tuba milkweed | AL, FL, GA, NC, SC, TX |
| * | *Asclepias tuberosa* | Butterfly weed | AL, AR, AZ, CA, CO, CT, DC, DE, FL, GA, IA, IL, IN, KS, KY, LA, MA, MD, ME (Possibly Extirpated), MI, MN, MO, MS, NC, NE, NH (Endangered), NJ, NM, NY (Exploitably Vulnerable), OH, OK, PA, RI (Special Concern), SC, SD, TN, TX, UT, VA, VT (Threatened), WI, WV and ON, QC (Canada) |
| | *Asclepias uncialis* | Wheel milkweed | AZ, CO, NM, NV, OK, UT, TX, WY |
| * | *Asclepias variegata* | Redring milkweed | AL, AR, CT (Endangered), DC, DE, FL, GA, IL, IN, KY, LA, MD, MO, MS, NC, NJ, NY (Endangered), OH, OK, PA (Endangered), SC, TN, TX, VA, WV and ON (Canada) |
| * | *Asclepias verticillata* | Whorled milkweed | AL, AR, AZ, CT, DC, DE, FL, GA, IA, IL, IN, KS, KY, LA, MA (Threatened), MD, MI, MN, MO, MS, MT, NC, ND, NE, NJ, NM, NY, OH, OK, PA, RI (Special Concern), SC, SD, TN, TX, VA, VT, WI, WV, WY and MB, ON, SK (Canada) |
| * * | *Asclepias vestita* | Woolly milkweed | CA |
| * | *Asclepias viridiflora* | Green comet milkweed | AL, AR, AZ, CT (Special Concern), DC, DE, FL (Endangered), GA, IA, IL, IN, KS, KY, LA, MD, MI, MN, MO, MS, MT, NC, ND, NE, NJ, NM, NY (Threatened), OH, OK, PA, SC, SD, TN, TX, VA, WI, WV and AB, BC, MB, ON, SK (Canada) |

| | | | |
|---|---|---|---|
| * | *Asclepias viridis* | Green antelope horn milkweed | AL, AR, FL, GA, IL, IN (Endangered), KS, KY, LA, MO, MS, NE, OH, OK, SC, TN, TX, WV |
| | *Asclepias viridula* | Southern milkweed | AL, FL (Threatened), GA |
| | *Asclepias welshii* | Welsh's milkweed | AZ, UT - Federally Threatened |
| *** | *Ampelamus laevis/ Cynanchum laeve* | Honey vine, smooth swallow-wort | AL, AR, DC, FL, GA, IA, ID, IL, IN, KS, KY, LA, MD, MO, MS, NC, NE, NY, OH, OK, PA (Endangered), SC, TN, TX, VA, WV |
| | **USDA Plants Database** | | http://plants.usda.gov |

---

| | | | |
|---|---|---|---|
| * | **Recommended for habitat** | Eastern U.S. | http://www.fs.fed.us/wildflowers/pollinators/ Monarch_Butterfly/habitat/milkweed_list.shtml |
| ** | **Recommended for habitat** | Western U.S. | |
| *** | **Listed as noxious weed in some states** | | |

## Non-native monarch host plants

These plants are all members of the *Asclepiadaceae* family and are grown in the U.S. and Canada, but are not native. Most are grown as annuals as they are not hardy in colder climates. With the exception of *Asclepias curassavica,* these plants may or may not be attractive to monarchs for laying eggs. Please note that it is always preferable to provide native milkweeds for monarchs.

| | | |
|---|---|---|
| *Asclepias curassavica* | Tropical milkweed | Not native to the U.S. or Canada – mostly grown as an annual |
| *Calotropis gigantea* | Giant milkweed, crown flower | Not native to the U.S. or Canada – mostly grown as an annual |
| *Calotropis procera* | Milkweed tree | Not native to the U.S. or Canada – mostly grown as an annual |
| *Gomphocarpus fruticosas* | Swan milkweed | Not native to the U.S. or Canada – mostly grown as an annual |
| *Gomphocarpus physocarpus* | Hairy balls, balloon plant | Not native to the U.S. or Canada – mostly grown as an annual |
| *Oxypetalum coeruleum* | Tweedia, Southern star, true blue milkweed | Not native to the U.S. or Canada – mostly grown as an annual |

# Where to Buy Milkweed Seeds & Plants

**American Meadows Nursery** (seeds and plants): americanmeadows.com

**Botanical Interests** (seeds) botanicalinterests.com

**Monarch Watch Milkweed Market** (seeds and plants): monarchwatch.org/milkweed/market

**Native Seed Network:** nativeseednetwork.org

**Prairie Moon Nursery** (seeds and plants): prairiemoon.com

**Shady Oak Butterfly Farm:** butterfliesetc.com/host-and-nectar-plants

**SmartSeeds:** etsy.com/shop/SmartSeeds

**Southwest Monarch Study** (seeds and plants): swmonarchs.org/nurseries.php

**Xerces Society Milkweed Seed Finder** (seeds): xerces.org/milkweed-seed-finder

# Nectar Plants for Pollinators

This list is by no means exhaustive, but these are plants that monarchs habitually gather nourishment from, later in the season. Bloom times are approximate and will vary according to your climate and location.

| Common Name | Botanical Name | Bloom Time | USDA Zone |
|---|---|---|---|
| Aster | *Symphyotrichum* spp. | Late Summer to Early Fall | 3-9 |
| Bergamot or Bee balm | *Monarda* spp. | Late Spring to Early Fall | 3-9 |
| Black-eyed Susan | *Rudbeckia hirta* | Mid-Summer to Early Fall | 3-9 |
| Blanket flower | *Gaillardia* spp. | Mid-Summer to Mid-Fall | 3-9 |
| Blazing star | *Liatris* spp. | Mid-Summer to Early Fall | 3-10 |
| Blue mistflower | *Conoclinium coelestinum* | Late Summer to Mid-Fall | 5-9 |
| Brazilian verbena | *Verbena bonariensis* | Mid-Summer to Mid-Fall | 7-10 |
| Brown-eyed Susan | *Rudbeckia triloba* | Late Summer to Mid-Fall | 3-11 |
| Butterfly bush | *Buddleia davidii* | Mid-Summer to Mid-Fall | 5-10 |
| Buttonbush | *Cephalanthus occidentalis* | Mid-Summer to Early Fall | 5-10 |
| Common milkweed | *Asclepias syriaca* | Mid-Summer | 4-9 |
| Coneflower | *Echinacea* spp. | Mid-Summer to Mid-Fall | 2-10 |
| Fleabane | *Erigeron* spp. | Late Spring to Mid-Summer | 2-9 |
| Flowering sage | *Salvia* spp. | Mid-Summer to Mid-Fall | 7-9 |
| Goldenrod | *Solidago* spp. | Late Summer to Early Fall | 3-8 |
| Hyssop | *Agastache* spp. | Late Summer to Early Fall | 4-9 |
| Ironweed | *Vernonia* spp. | Late Summer to Early Fall | 5-9 |
| Joe Pye weed | *Eutrochium maculatum* | Mid-Summer to Early Fall | 3-8 |
| Maximillian sunflower | *Helianthus maximilianii* | Late Summer to Mid-Fall | 4-10 |
| Mexican sunflower | *Tithonia rotundifolia* | Mid-Summer to Mid-Fall | Annual |
| Signet marigold | *Tagetes tenuifolia* | Mid-Summer to Mid-Fall | Annual |
| Sneezeweed | *Helenium autumnale* | Late Summer to Mid-Fall | 3-8 |
| Stonecrop sedum | *Hylotelephium spectabile* | Late Summer to Mid-Fall | 3-9 |
| Sulphur cosmos | *Cosmos sulphureus* | Mid-Summer to Mid-Fall | Annual |
| Summersweet | *Clethra alnifolia* | Mid-Summer to Mid-Fall | 3-9 |
| Tickseed | *Coreopsis* spp. | Mid-Summer to Early Fall | 3-8 |
| Yarrow | *Achillea millefolium* | Late Spring to Mid-Fall | 3-9 |
| Zinnia | *Zinnia* spp. | Mid-Summer to Mid-Fall | Annual |

# More Milkweed Insects You May Encounter

Besides the insects shown in the Predators at Large chapter, there are a number of other insects that share an affinity for milkweed plants – and you might be concerned about some of them. But just remember this: Most of them are more of a nuisance than a problem, unless you have a heavy infestation. What's heavy? When you start to see the plant suffering a decline in health, it might be time to take some action.

> **Never use any kind of pesticide or chemical in an attempt to rid your milkweed plants of pests, not even those labeled as organic. They nearly always will harm or kill monarchs and other beneficial insects.**

## What to do about unwelcome insects

All of the insects listed below feed on the milkweed plant in some manner or another, and in most cases, they can co-exist with the monarchs just fine. Sometimes though, they may affect the health of the milkweed plants, so you many want to find a way to remove them from your plants.

The milkweed bugs and beetles will generally drop off the plant when disturbed, so shaking the plant is usually effective. You can also use a hose sprayer to knock them off.

In the case of tiny aphids, which suck the sap from leaves and leave a sticky "honeydew," you may need to be a little more aggressive and use your fingers to rub them off the leaves. If you're lucky, ladybug larvae or adults will come along and do the job for you. Aphids are one of their favorite snacks.

**Milkweed longhorn beetle** (*Tetraopes* **spp.**)

As their name suggests, these hard-shelled beetles can have extremely long antennae. They too, have the orange and black coloring of most milkweed insects. There are 13 species of these beetles in North America and their appearances are similar. They feed on the milkweed plant and generally spend their entire life on it.

**Swamp milkweed leaf beetle**
*(Labidomera clivicollis)*

The first time I saw one of these, I thought to myself, "That's one big fat ladybug!" And that's just what it looks like – a ladybug on steroids. These beetles feed on leaves and drop to the ground when disturbed, like most of their beetle friends.

## Milkweed bugs

These are probably the bugs you'll see most often on your milkweed. They're deep orange and black – that familiar aposematic appearance that says, "Don't eat me! I'm poisonous and I taste bad!" They're often seen in clusters, especially when they're young. They feed on the milkweed and generally don't bother with monarchs.

There are two different species of them: the small milkweed bug *(Lygaeus kalmii)* and the large milkweed bug *(Oncopeltus fasciatus)*. The latter is the one most commonly seen in the biggest part of the Eastern population of the monarch's summer breeding range. They feed on the milkweed plant, but they especially like milkweed seeds, so you'll often see them congregating in the fall on and around the seed pods. The small milkweed bug has a black "X" formation on its back, while the large milkweed bug will have a horizontal black bar across its back.

Milkweed bugs are often mistaken for Eastern box elder bugs *(Boisea trivittata)*, which also have the dark orange (often more red) and black coloring.

### Aphids (*Aphis nerii*)

Aphids are one of the tiniest insects you may see congregating on your milkweed plants. They appear as clusters of tiny, pearly-yellow bugs on stems, buds and almost always near tender new growth. They're a sucking insect and leave a sticky substance called honeydew in their wake. Aphids can weaken and disfigure a milkweed plant if there are enough of them present. They are commonly called oleander aphids.

### Milkweed tussock moth caterpillars (*Euchaetes egle*)

I think these guys are pretty darn cute. They're like little fuzzy teddy bears sporting the same colors as the adult monarch butterfly. That's no accident, because their predators know to leave those colors alone. They taste bad too! Also called milkweed tiger moth, you'll find their larvae crawling on milkweed and dogbane leaves from mid-to-late summer.

As young caterpillars, they can be found in groups and they'll pretty much devour everything in their path, including monarch eggs and tiny caterpillars. As larger caterpillars, they're more often found singly. They don't eat the entire milkweed leaf but rather "skeletonize" the leaves, leaving a lacy framework behind.

# Where Can I Visit Monarchs at Their Overwintering Sites?

## Eastern population

The Eastern population that spends its winter in Mexico occupies approximately 12 colonies there. The colonies are located in the states of Michoacán and Mexico, about 60-75 miles northwest of Mexico City. Four of them are open to the public. You can visit independently or as part of a tour group (recommended). A Google search of "visiting monarch sanctuaries in Mexico" will yield links to many informative sites, including those for making travel plans.

Because the sanctuaries are in steep mountains nearly two miles above sea level, it's recommended that you be in good physical shape at the time of your visit. Altitude sickness may be a factor and there will be climbing of narrow trails involved, though at some locations there will be horses to rent for part of the ascent.

### Michoacán
El Rosario, near Ocampo
Sierra Chincua, near Angangueo

### Estado de Mexico
Cerro Pelon, near Zitacuaro
Piedra Herrada, near Valle de Bravo

## Western population

The Western populations of the monarch butterfly overwinter along the California coast and make up about 5% of the total worldwide monarch population. The best time to view them is late October through January. There are over 200 sites, which can shift over the years, but the following California sites have remained constant, though density may vary. Some locations may have park rangers or docents available.

### Sonoma County
Bodega Dunes Campground, Bodega Bay

### Marin County
Terrace Ave., Bolinas
Fort Baker, Sausalito

### Alameda County
Albany Hill, Albany
Ardenwood Historical Farm, Fremont

### Santa Cruz County
Lighthouse Field State Beach, Santa Cruz
Natural Bridges State Beach, Santa Cruz

### Monterey County
Andrew Molera State Park
Butterfly Grove Sanctuary, Pacific Grove
Point Lobos State Park, Carmel Bay

**San Luis Obispo County**
Halcyon Hill, Halcyon
Oceano Campground, Oceano
North Beach Campground, Pismo Beach

**Santa Barbara County**
Ellwood Main, Goleta
Gaviota State Beach, Gaviota
Gaviota Gas Plant, Gaviota

**Ventura County**
Big Sycamore Canyon, Pt. Mugu State Park
Camino Real Park, Ventura
Ocean Ave. Park, Ventura

**Los Angeles County**
El Dorado Nature Center, Long Beach
Recreation Park (south), Long Beach
Woodlawn Cemetery, Santa Monica

**Orange County**
Golden West College, Huntington Beach
Huntington Central Park, Huntington Beach
San Clemente State Beach, San Clemente

**San Diego County**
Grape Street Park, Balboa Park
Presidio Park, Old Town
UCSD Coast Site, Azul St.

Maps for these locations can be found at
The Monarch Program website:
**monarchprogram.org/where-to-see-overwintering-monarchs**

Additional information for California
overwintering sites is located on the
Xerces Society website:
**xerces.org/where-to-see-monarchs-in-california**

# Where Can I Donate?

**Monarch Watch**
monarchwatch.org/donate

**Monarch Joint Venture**
monarchjointventure.org/get-involved/donate

**University of Minnesota Monarch Lab –
Monarch Conservation & Education Fund**
monarchlab.org/donate

**Pollinator Partnership –
Monarch Wings Across America**
pollinatorpartnership.org

**The Monarch Program**
(aka **California Monarch Studies, Inc.**)
monarchprogram.org/how-to-donate-funds

**Live Monarch Foundation**
livemonarch.org/donation.htm

**Save Our Monarchs Foundation**
saveourmonarchs.org/store/c2/
Make_a_Donation

**Forests for Monarchs**
forestsformonarchs.org/donate

**Southwest Monarch Study**
swmonarchs.org/support.php

**Monarch Butterfly Fund**
monarchconservation.org

**Wild Ones – Wild for Monarchs**
wildones.org/learn/wild-for-monarchs

**World Wildlife Fund – Adopt a Monarch Butterfly**
gifts.worldwildlife.org/gift-center/gifts/
Species-Adoptions/Monarch-Butterfly

**Center for Biological Diversity**
biologicaldiversity.org

## In Canada:

**David Suzuki Foundation**
davidsuzuki.org

**Canadian Wildlife Federation**
cwf-fcf.org/en/explore-our-
work/endangered-species/
help-the-monarchs

*Disclaimer: Listing here does not imply endorsement. These are just some of the many opportunities available for donating to help monarchs. As always, be sure your money goes to the work for which it's intended. Don't overlook local opportunities.*

# Books, Films & Helpful Websites

## Books

### Non-fiction

*Chasing Monarchs: Migrating with the Butterflies of Passage* by Robert Michael Pyle. 1999, Houghton Mifflin Harcourt.

*An Extraordinary Life: The Story of a Monarch Butterfly* by Laurence Pringle. 1997, Orchard Books.

*Four Wings and a Prayer: Caught in the Mystery of the Monarch Butterfly* by Sue Halpern. 2001, Pantheon.

*The Last Monarch Butterfly: Conserving the Monarch Butterfly in a Brave New World* by Phil Schappert.  2004, Firefly Books.

*Milkweed, Monarchs, and More: A Field Guide to the Invertebrate Community in the Milkweed Patch (2nd Ed.)* by Ba Rea, Karen Oberhauser, Michael A. Quinn. 2010, Bas Relief, LLC.

*Monarchs in a Changing World: Biology and Conservation of an Iconic Butterfly* edited by Karen S. Oberhauser, Kelly R. Nail, Sonia Altizer. 2015, Cornell University Press.

### Fiction

*The Butterfly's Daughter* by Mary Alice Monroe. 2011, Gallery Books.

*Flight Behavior* by Barbara Kingsolver. 2012, Harper.

### Youth

*Flight of the Butterflies* (Penguin Young Readers, Level 3) by Roberta Edwards. Penguin Young Readers, 2010. Ages 6-8; Grades 1-3.

*Gotta Go! Gotta Go!* (Sunburst Book) by Sam Swope. 2004, Square Fish. Ages 3-6; Pre-school - 1.

*How to Raise Monarch Butterflies: A Step-by-Step Guide for Kids* by Carol Pasternak. Firefly Books, 2012. Age 6-12 years; Grades 1-7.

*Monarch and Milkweed* by Helen Frost. Atheneum Books for Young Readers, 2008. Ages 3-8; Grades Pre-school - 3.

*Monarch Magic! Butterfly Activities & Nature Discoveries* by Lynn Rosenblatt. Williamson Pub, 1998. Ages 8-11; Grades 3-6.

*Mr. McGinty's Monarchs* by Linda Vander Heyden. Sleeping Bear Press, 2016. Ages 6-9; Grades 1-4.

*Velma Gratch and the Way Cool Butterfly* by Alan Madison. Schwartz & Wade, 2007. Ages 4-8; Grades Pre-school-3.

*When Butterflies Cross the Sky: The Monarch Butterfly Migration (Extraordinary Migrations)* by Sharon Katz Cooper. 2015, Picture Window Books. Ages 5-9; Grades K-4.

## Films

**Flight of the Butterflies** (IMAX) directed by Mike Slee. 2016, Shout! Factory.

**The Incredible Journey of the Butterflies** by NOVA. 2007, PBS Home Video.

**The Incredible Story of the Monarch Butterfly: Four Wings and a Prayer** directed by Nick de Pencier. 2007, Primitive Entertainment.

**Metamorphosis: The Beauty and Design of Butterflies** directed by Lad Allen. 2011, Illustra Media.

## Websites

**Monarch Watch** – monarchwatch.org

**Journey North** – learner.org/jnorth/monarch

**Monarch Joint Venture** – monarchjointventure.org

**Monarch Lab** – monarchlab.org

**Make Way for Monarchs** – makewayformonarchs.org

**The Xerces Society** – xerces.org/monarchs

**The Beautiful Monarch** (Public group on Facebook with 11,000+ members) – facebook.com/groups/TheBeautifulMonarch

**Texas Butterfly Ranch** – texasbutterflyranch.com

**Butterfly Fun Facts** – butterflyfunfacts.com

**Monarch Butterfly Garden** – monarchbutterflygarden.net

# Bibliography

## Books

*The Last Monarch Butterfly: Conserving the Monarch Butterfly in a Brave New World,* by Phil Schappert. 2004, Firefly Books.

*Milkweed, Monarchs and More: A Field Guide to the Invertebrate Community in the Milkweed Patch (2nd Ed.),* by Ba Rea, Karen Oberhauser, and Michael A. Quinn. 2010, Bas Relief, LLC.

*The Monarch Butterfly,* by F.A. Urquhart. 1960, University of Toronto Press.

*Monarchs in a Changing World: Biology and Conservation of an Iconic Butterfly,* edited by Karen S. Oberhauser, Kelly R. Nail, and Sonia Altizer. 2015, Cornell University Press.

## Websites

The Center for Biological Diversity – biologicaldiversity.org/species/invertebrates/monarch_butterfly

Journey North – learner.org/jnorth/monarch

Monarch Joint Venture – monarchjointventure.org

Monarch Watch – monarchwatch.org

Pollinators of Native Plants – pollinatorsnativeplants.com

The University of Minnesota Monarch Lab – monarchlab.org

USDA Natural Resources Conservation Service PLANTS database – plants.usda.gov

Xerces Society – xerces.org

# Index

# Acknowledgments

When I decided to write this book, I knew what lay ahead for me, and so did my family. They'd been through it before with my first book, *Indoor Plant Décor: The Design Stylebook for Houseplants*, co-authored with my good friend, Jenny Peterson. But no one truly understands what it's like to live with an author with a deadline more than my husband, Romie. Nearly 42 years of marriage is an asset, because he knew that when I was crabby because things weren't coming together like I'd like, it was me, not him. And the fact that he was willing to fend for himself for days (weeks!) on end without complaint speaks volumes about his love and support. They don't come any better.

Though I'm an incessant self-learner, my knowledge about the monarch could never have reached the level it has without so many others: in particular, the people at Monarch Watch and the Dplex-L email group, Journey North, Monarch Joint Venture, Dr. Lincoln Brower, Edith Smith, and Monika Maeckle.

I want to especially thank Holli Hearn, founder of The Beautiful Monarch Facebook Group. Holli has built a wonderful resource and community there, which is over 11,000 strong as of this writing. She is tireless in her dedication to educating and helping others learn more about the monarch, and doesn't get a dime for doing it. That just doesn't seem right.

Thank you to Paul Kelly, of St. Lynn's Press, who was once again willing to invest in me and my vision for a book. I can't say enough good about my editor, Cathy Dees, and my graphic designer, Holly Rosborough. This is the second time I've worked with this team, and they were phenomenal as always. They never lose their patience (not visibly anyway!) and are especially respectful of an author's voice and dreams for their own book. Thanks, too, to Chloe Wertz for working hard at getting the word out to the world about *The Monarch*.

I appreciate the support of the following, and I sure hope I haven't left anyone out (if I did, I didn't mean to): Jenny Peterson, Christina Salwitz, Robin Haglund, Karen Chapman, Judy Seaborn of Botanical Interests, Diana Kirby, Beth Stetenfeld, Julie Adolf, Joe Lamp'l and the "Growing a Greener World" team, Mary Galea and Laura Davies Adams at The Pollinator Partnership, Robin Horton, Shawna Coronado, and my mom, Louise Hartwig.

Special thanks to Daniel Gasteiger, whose inspiration to me is known only by him, and whom I hope one day to meet, so that I can express my gratitude in person.

I have a great appreciation for our Creator, who really outdid Himself with the magnificent monarchs. I hope and pray that they fly in great numbers again so that my grandchildren and their grandchildren can experience the wonder of it all.

## A final word . . .

Well, let's hope there isn't ever a final word on monarchs. But I do need to mention the following:

I have done my best to do right by this amazing insect, one that I love so much. I have spent countless hours, days, weeks and months researching the monarch and made a great effort to be sure that what I have presented here is as accurate as possible for me to do. I'm sure I became quite annoying to Dr. Lincoln Brower, one of the world's foremost authorities on monarchs, in my quest for details, but he humored me in my persistence and came through for me. I'm grateful for and humbled by the time he devoted to someone who wasn't one of his university students, or anyone he'd ever even heard of before, and I take full responsibility for any factual errors.

Scientists and biologists and those who study the natural world don't always agree, and in a few instances, when I came upon conflicting information from equally sound sources, I had to make a judgment call in the way that I presented the material. Sometimes it seemed best to go with the simple explanation. More is being discovered about this incredible creature all the time and more mysteries solved, so I urge you to never stop learning about it. I know I won't.

# About the Author

**KYLEE BAUMLE** is a citizen scientist who participates in several programs that provide data to researchers studying monarchs (through Monarch Watch with the University of Kansas, and Journey North, which reports migration sightings, roosts and other key monarch data). Her rural Ohio garden is a Certified Monarch Waystation (#948) since 2006, a Certified Wildlife Habitat, and is registered with Pollinator Partnership as part of The Million Pollinator Garden Challenge.

A lifelong gardener and photographer with an endless curiosity about nature, Kylee is a regular columnist for both her local newspaper and Ohio Gardener magazine. She has also written for Horticulture, The American Gardener, Fine Gardening and Indiana Gardener magazines. Her photography has appeared in Fine Gardening and in numerous books, magazines, garden industry trade publications and catalogs. In addition to *The Monarch*, she is co-author of *Indoor Plant Décor*.

Discovering the unique and beautiful monarch butterfly has helped Kylee appreciate how so many things in nature depend on so many other things, including human beings. She believes that each and every one of us who share this earth can make a difference when we work together and fulfill the potential that we all possess to do good. Kylee wants her grandchildren to not only be able to tell the wondrous story of the monarch to their own children and grandchildren, but to be able to show them much of it firsthand.

You can follow Kylee's blog, Our Little Acre (ourlittleacre.com), where she writes about her love for the natural world. 🦋

# OTHER BOOKS FROM ST. LYNN'S PRESS

www.stlynnspress.com

### Good Bug Bad Bug
by Jessica Walliser
104 pages • Hardback
ISBN: 978-0981961590

### Cool Flowers
by Lisa Mason Ziegler
160 pages • Paperback
ISBN: 978-0989268813

### The Cocktail Hour Garden
by C.L. Fornari
192 pages, Hardback
ISBN: 978-1943366026

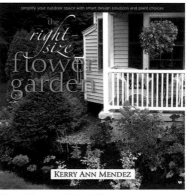

### The Right-Size Flower Garden
by Kerry Ann Mendez
192 pages • Hardback
ISBN: 978-0989268875